THE BIG BOOK OF

Stickelers [sic]

First published in the USA in 2006 by
Fair Winds Press, a member of
Quayside Publishing Group
33 Commercial Street
Gloucester, MA 01930

10 09 08 07 06   1 2 3 4 5

ISBN - 13: 978-1-59233-225-0
ISBN - 10: 1-59233-225-0

Library of Congress Cataloging-in-Publication Data available

Cover design by Peter King & Company
Book design by King Features Syndicate, Inc. and Fair Winds Press

Printed and bound in USA

THE BIG BOOK OF

Stickelers [sic]

320 Fun and Challenging Brainteasers to Sharpen Your Mind

TERRY STICKELS

FAIR WINDS
PRESS
GLOUCESTER, MASSACHUSETTS

FOREWORD

When Glenn Mott and Brendan Burford of King Features and I first discussed doing a syndicated newspaper puzzle called STICKELERS, our goal was to create a fun and challenging array of puzzles that required readers to use a wide spectrum of thinking skills. We knew we would have puzzle solvers from ages six to 106, from first graders to physicists, and that it would take a juggling act of large proportions to please the maximum number of solvers. The end result was a creative smattering of spatial/visual puzzles, logic puzzles, wordplay, and math puzzles that now appear daily in newspapers across America, the best of which are collected here, for you, in *The Big Book of STICKELERS [sic]*.

The best part about our STICKELERS is that anyone can do them! No academic qualifications are needed, just a brain and a sense of lighthearted fun.

It's now our third year of publishing this puzzle in syndication and every year the number of dedicated fans grows and a new batch of STICKELERS addicts are born. We have always stayed true to our initial principle of providing something for everyone, so you can be sure that something in this book will catch your fancy. There are almost no limitations to the kinds of puzzles that qualify as STICKELERS, so you might encounter puzzles here that you've never seen before—puzzles that force you to think and solve in a whole new way! We're breaking new ground all the time and yet I can honestly say that we still haven't scratched the surface.

Now, it's time for you to have some fun. I hope the puzzles that follow challenge you and make you smile at the same time. There is no set way to do these puzzles, and you don't have to start at the beginning. Start in the middle and move around; begin a puzzle and come back at a later time; be flexible in your thinking pursuits, try different approaches and tactics.

Whatever your methods, enjoy the cranial adventure you're about to embark upon.

Happy solving,

Terry Stickels

www.terrystickels.com

HOW TO FIND THE ANSWERS

When you're finished with a puzzle, simply flip the page to find the correct solution. The solutions to puzzles on left-hand pages appear beneath puzzles on the next left-hand pages, and the same goes for puzzles on right-hand pages. (That is, except for the solutions to the last two puzzles, which appear beneath the first two puzzles in the book.)

Below are six cirlces which have a pattern beginning with circle one. Can you figure out the pattern and fill in circle six?

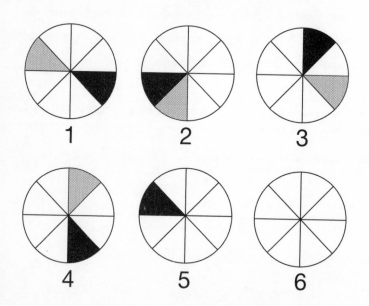

Answer to page 327

The one word that completes the others
is **TIME**.

by Terry Stickels

Can you figure out the sequence
below? Try to fill in the
question-marked boxes with the
appropriate number of dots.

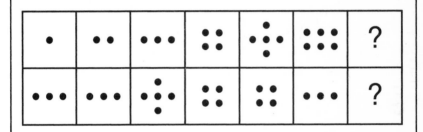

Answer to page 328

The next number is **8008**.

STICKELERS [sic].

by**Terry Stickels**

Which of the following patterns below does not belong with the rest?

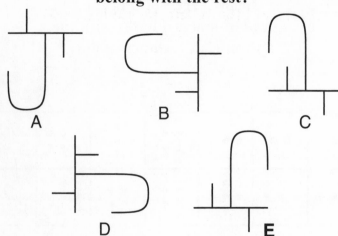

A

B

C

D

E

Answer to page 8

The figure to the left shows how circle six should look. Each black section moves clockwise three spaces from circle to circle; each shaded section moves counter-clockwise two spaces from circle to circle. Circle five has only black section because both shaded and solid are on the same spot.

by**Terry Stickels** [sic].

Each of the letter circles below spell out a word. Can you determine the logic of the two wheels and figure out the hidden word for each?

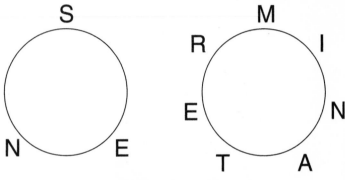

Answer to page 9

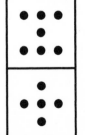

The bottom row of dots represent the number of letters used to spell the number of dots in the top row.

What should the next figure in the sequence below look like?

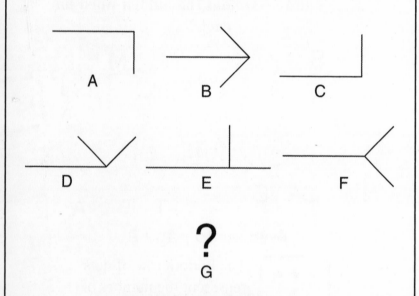

A

B

C

D

E

F

?

G

Answer to page 10

Figure **C** does not belong.
Figures A, B, and D contain the letter "J."
Figure C contains a backward "J."

STICKELERS [sic].

by**Terry Stickels**

The letters in the box below are strung together in such a way that they spell out a common word. Can you figure out the word?

S	M	E
E	M	R
E	Z	I

Answer to page 11

Circle one spells: SENSE
Circle two spells: TERMINATE

by Terry Stickels

What number belongs in the middle of the last triangle?

23 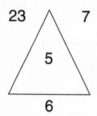 7

5

6

-8 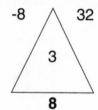 32

3

8

2 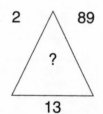 89

?

13

Answer to page 12

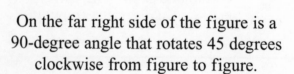

On the far right side of the figure is a 90-degree angle that rotates 45 degrees clockwise from figure to figure.

by**Terry Stickels**

What number should replace the question mark? Hint: The logic is "verticle," not horizontal.

7	2	13
21	8	65
84	40	390
420	240	?

Answer to page 13

The word is MESMERIZE. It starts with the "M" in the middle of the square, moves to the "E" to the left, then moves clockwise around the square.

by **Terry Stickels**

Below is a number pyramid that when completed will have the numbers 1 thru 15. The interesting feature of this puzzle is that each number directly below any two numbers must be the difference of those two numbers. Can you fill in the blanks?

Example:

6 2 5

4 3

1

13 __ 15 __ 6

__ __ __ __

__ __ __

__ __

__

Answer to page 14

The number 7 should go in the middle of the last triangle. For each triangle, add the top two numbers and divide by the bottom number to arrive at the middle number.

 [sic].

byTerry Stickels

How many squares of any size are in the figure below?

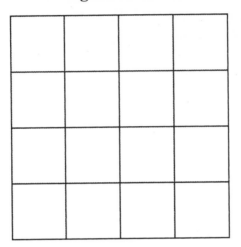

Answer to page 15

In the first column, 21 is found by multiplying 7 by 3, then 21 is multiplied by 4, and 84 is multiplied by 5. . . In the second column, 2 is multiplied by 4, 8 by 5, and 40 by 6. . . The third column starts with multiplying 13 by 5, 65 by 6, and 390 by 7, making the answer 2,730.

by **Terry Stickels**

Below are three squares of the same size and dimension. Can you put them together to create seven squares? The seven squares do not have to be the same size.

Answer to page 16

13 3 15 14 **6**
10 12 1 8
2 11 7
9 4
5

by**Terry Stickels**

What number should replace the question mark in the last box?

13		7
	71	
8		2

4		1
	24	
11		9

5		8
	39	
3		10

12		4
	?	
6		14

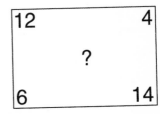

Answer to page 17

There are **30** squares in the figure.

How many four-sided figures are in the figure below?

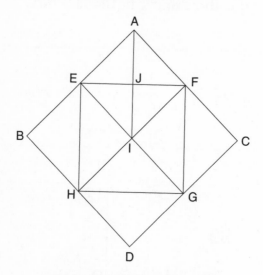

Answer to page 18

How many four-sided figures are in the figure below?

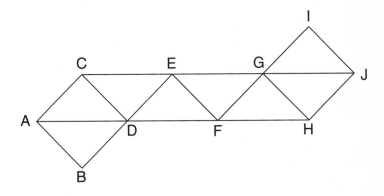

Answer to page 19

The middle number of each box can be found by multiplying the number in the bottom left-hand corner by the number in the upper right-hand corner and then adding that to the sum of the other two numbers, making the answer 50.

STICKELERS [sic].

by Terry Stickels

Below are five figures, and one is different
from the others. Can you figure out
which one doesn't belong?

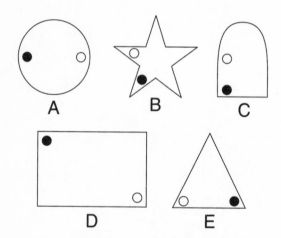

A   B   C

D   E

Answer to page 20

There are **23** four-sided figures. They are:

ABDC	ABHI	AIGF	BHFE	CFEG	EHGF
AEIF	AIGC	BDGE	CFIG	DGIH	EHIJ
ABHF	AEHF	BHGE	CFHD	DGFH	FJIG
AEGC	AEHI	BHIE	CFHG	DGEH	

What number should logically replace the question mark in the third triangle?

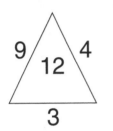

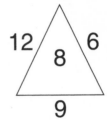

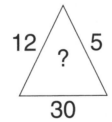

Answer to page 21

There are **18** four-sided figures. They are:

AHGC	ABEC	CDFE	CDHJ	DEJH	FGJH
AFEC	ADEC	CDHG	DEGH	EFHG	FIJH
ABDC	ACJH	CDFG	DEGF	EFHJ	GHJI

by **Terry Stickels**

In the grid below, place the numbers 1 through 8 so that no number is next to a consecutive one in the counting sequence (horizontally, vertically, or diagonally).

12			10
9			11

Answer to page 22

Figure **C** does not belong. Each figure can be divided symmetrically with a dot in each half except figure **C**.

by Terry Stickels

Which letter logically belongs where the question mark is in the fifth triangle below?

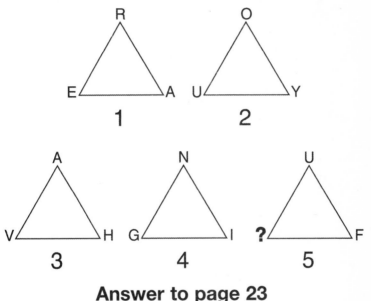

Answer to page 23

The answer is **2**. If you multiply the top two numbers in each respective triangle and divide by the bottom number, you get the result in the middle of the triangle.

by **Terry Stickels**

Below are six letters, where one is different from
the others. Can you figure out which letter doesn't
belong? (Disregard the fact that A is the only vowel,
and that it forms an enclosed shape.)

A F H K N T

Answer to page 24

Here's one answer. Did you find another?

12	4	6	10
7	1	8	2
9	3	5	11

One of the figures below does not belong with the others. Can you determine the logic of the figures and pick the one that is different from the others? Hint: The answer has nothing to do with symmetry.

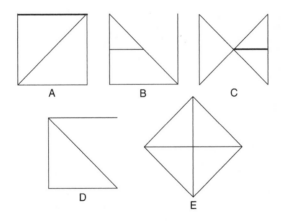

A   B   C

D   E

Answer to page 25

The answer is **N**. Starting with the first triangle and reading counterclockwise in each triangle, the puzzle spells out, "ARE YOU HAVING FUN?"

What should the question-marked box look like in the sequence below?

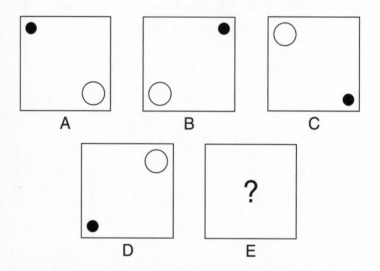

Answer to page 26

The letter **T** does not belong. All of the other letters are created by making 3 separate, straight strokes.

The letters in the figure below are strung together in a logical way which spells a common word. Can you figure out the word?

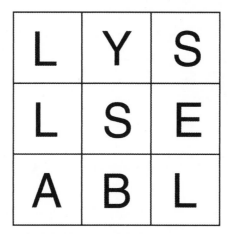

Answer to page 27

D does not belong. All of the figures have a "Z" shape in them except figure **D**.

**Would the letter "P" go above or below
the line in the figure below?**

A   F   H I J K L M N O
_____

  B C D E G

Answer to page 28

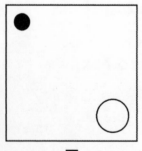

E

It should look just like the first box. The pattern is that the small black dot and the white circle each move clockwise to the next corner of the square.

There is a certain logic determining the numbers in the grid below. Can you figure out the logic and fill in the question-marked box in grid "D"?

9	5
15	27

A

0	1
3	0

B

6	12
36	18

C

15	2
6	?

D

Answer to page 29

The word is SYLLABLES. Starting with the "S" in the upper right-hand corner, move counter-clockwise around the outside of the square until you finish with the middle "S." You can also start with the middle "S," move to the "Y," and continue counterclockwise from there.

by**Terry Stickels**

There is an old puzzle that asks if you can form seven matchsticks into three triangles. The answer looks like this:

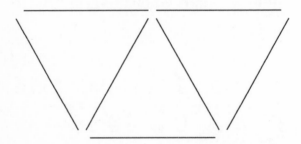

Now here is a new puzzle. Using six matchsticks, see if you can create five triangles.

Answer to page 30

The letter "P" should go below the line, as it rhymes with the other letters below the line, but not those above the line.

What number should logically replace the question mark in the third box?

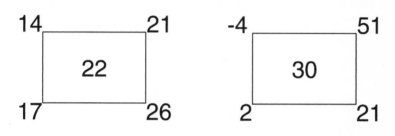

14 _____ 21

22

17 _____ 26

-4 _____ 51

30

2 _____ 21

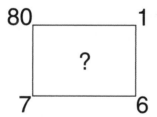

80 _____ 1

?

7 _____ 6

Answer to page 31

You must first multiply each top number by three and place the result in the diagonal box, making the answer **45**.

by**Terry Stickels**

The capital letters C, O, S, and U hold a distinction among all other capital letters. Can you figure out what the distinction is?

C O S U

Answer to page 32

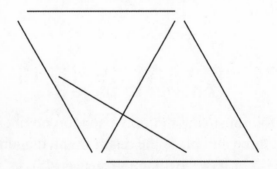

by Terry Stickels

In a magic square, the rows, columns, and diagonals all add up to the same total. The numbers to be used are listed below the grid. See how long it takes you to come up with the correct placement of each number.

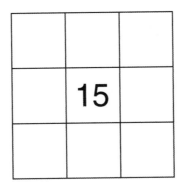

11, 12, 13, 14, 16, 17, 18, 19

Answer to page 33

The number **6** should replace the question mark.
The numbers in each group add up to 100.

by**Terry Stickels**

Four of the five words below share a common characteristic. Can you figure out which word doesn't belong?

1) REPAPER
2) ROTATOR
3) KAYAK
4) REDIVIDES
5) DEIFIED

Answer to page 34

The capital letters C, O, S, and U are the only capital letters that do not contain at least one straight line in their configuration.

STICKELERS [sic].

byTerry Stickels

The letters in the grid below are strung together in a logical way to spell a common word. Can you find the word?

I	O	N	A
L	U	L	I
L	M	T	R
I	M	I	E

Answer to page 35

Here's one way.

14	13	18
19	15	11
12	17	16

by**Terry Stickels**

**Four of the five figures below can be drawn
without lifting the pencil or crossing any other
lines. Which figure doesn't belong?**

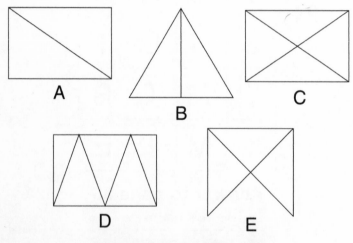

A

B

C

D

E

Answer to page 36

The fourth word, **REDIVIDES**, does not belong.
The other words are palindromes, which read the
same forward and backward.

Below is a square formed by using pennies
(8 total). Using the same pennies, can you create
a square that is 4 x 4?

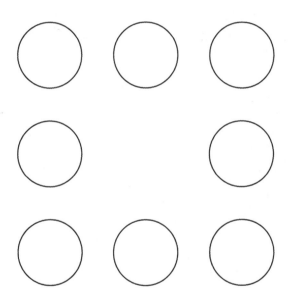

Answer to page 37

The word is **MULTIMILLIONAIRE**.

Can you figure out the next letter in the following sequence?

C F I L O R U ?

Answer to page 38

Figure **C** is the only one that cannot be drawn
without lifting the pencil or
crossing any other lines.

NOW   CRAM   ELVES

TALE   TRAIN   LATE

HOW   PEAR

Which of the words below fits best with the group of words above?

VAIN
CRIME
LAUNCH
WING
WILT

Answer to page 39

Simply place four of the pennies on top of the other four, and you've created a square that is 4 x 4.

One of the figures below cannot be folded into a cube. Can you figure out which one it is?

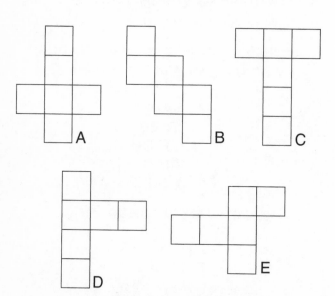

A

B

C

D

E

Answer to page 40

The sequence is every third letter of the alphabet, which makes the missing letter "X."

by**Terry Stickels**

The numbers in each set have a logical relationship. The relationships are the same for each of the six groups. Can you figure out the missing number in the sixth group?

3 3	27

4 2	16

4 4	256

1 5	1

2 6	64

5 1	?

Answer to page 41

WING is the best fit. Each of the words in the top group form a new word when an **S** is added to the front of it.

One of the figures below does not belong with the others. Can you figure out which one is different? Hint: The difference is a common, simple, very basic feature having to do with the figures' structures.

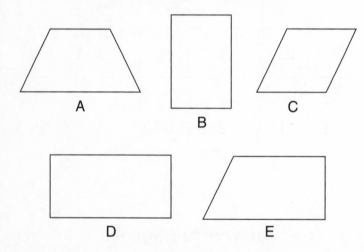

A

B

C

D

E

Answer to page 42

Figure **D** cannot be folded into a cube.

Here's a fun trick you can try on your friends:
Can you arrange 10 pennies into five rows of
four pennies each?

Answer to page 43

The missing number is **5**. When the second
number is treated as an exponent of the first,
you get the answer.

3^3	27		4^2	16		4^4	256
1^5	1		2^6	64		5^1	5

by Terry Stickels

Here is a fun analogy that has more to do
with your mental flexibility than the
meaning of the words. Can you figure out
the missing word?

EVIL is to VILE

as STOP is to ?

Answer to page 44

Figures **C** does not belong. It is the only
figure with all sides equal in length.

by Terry Stickels

In the diagram below, the same rules apply in each set of boxes to determine the number in each triangle. Can you figure out the missing number?

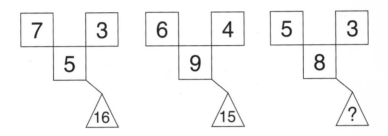

Answer to page 45

Here's how you arrange 10 pennies into 5 rows of 4 pennies each:

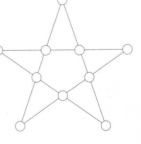

byTerry Stickels

Below are five sets of two letters. Can you figure out what the two missing letters should be?

N	D
J	F
M	A
M	J
J	A
?	?

Answer to page 46

The missing word is TOPS. The "E" in EVIL was simply moved to the end to create VILE. Likewise, the "S" in STOP moves to the end to create TOPS.

Each of the 2 letters below represents a different digit (not zero). Can you figure out which digits the J and the H represent?

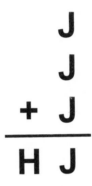

$$
\begin{array}{r}
J \\
J \\
+\ J \\
\hline
H\ J
\end{array}
$$

Answer to page 47

The missing number is 7. Multiply the numbers in the top 2 squares of each set, then subtract the number in the bottom square, and that will give you the number in the triangle.

The numbers **6009** and **6119** are both numbers that can be rotated 180 degrees and still read the same. Can you figure out the first number immediately preceding 6009 that holds this same characteristic? This is a fun one you can try on your friends to see who can solve it the quickest.

Answer to page 48

The missing letters are **S** and **O**. The sequence is the first letters of the months of the year, in order, starting with **N**ovember and **D**ecember.

by Terry Stickels

The following 11 letters unscrambled form a word.
Can you figure out the word?

B E D C U
E C L
N R
A M S

Answer to page 49

J can only be a **5**,
which makes the **H** a **1**.

There are five books side by side on a shelf. Their colors are gray, yellow, white, red, and black. The following information is known about the order of the books:

1. The yellow book is between the black and the red books.

2. The gray book is not first and the red book is not last.

3. The white book is separated from the red book by two books.

What is the position of the gray book? If the gray book is not next to the white book, what is the order of the five books from first to last?

Answer to page 50

The first number preceding 6009 that can be rotated 180 degress and still read the same is
1961.

The puzzle below is a form of syllogism used in logic. Is the conclusion TRUE or FALSE, based on the 3 statements?

Some PERX are DAFFS.
All DAFFS are GARTS.
Some GARTS are TINX.

Conclusion:
Some PERX are TINX.

Answer to page 51

Unscrambled, the letters form the word
UNSCRAMBLED.

Given the arrangement of the numbers below,
should the 11 be above or below the line?

1						8		
2	3	4	5	6	7	9	10	?

Answer to page 52

The gray book is in the last position on the
shelf. The order of the five books is: white,
black, yellow, red, then gray.

STICKELERS [sic].

by**Terry Stickels**

How many triangles are in the figure
to the right? Be careful and take
your time — there may be
more than you think.

A

E F

B

D

C

Answer to page 53

The answer is **FALSE**. Some PERX *may*
be TINX, but it is not definite.

by**Terry Stickels**

The nine letters in the box below spell a word
that logically can be deduced from the pattern it
creates within the grid.
What is the word?

C	I	G
A	L	O
L	L	Y

Answer to page 54

The 11 should go above the line. 1, 8,
and 11 have a vowel as their first letter;
the others begin with a consonant.

 [sic].

by**Terry Stickels**

Try this puzzle with a group of friends. The one to get the correct answer the quickest is the winner!

Bob bought a clock and some wrapping paper for a total of $55. The clock costs $54 more than the wrapping paper. Quick, how much did the wrapping paper cost?

Answer to page 55

There are **8** triangles, they are:

ABC	ACD
ABD	AEF
ABE	BCF
ABF	BDE

What number should logically replace the question mark in the last box?

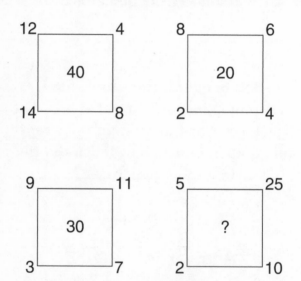

Answer to page 56

The letters spell the word LOGICALLY, starting with the middle "L" and continuing counterclockwise from the "O" to its right.

What number should logically replace the question mark in the diagram below?

3	5	1	10
8	7	9	11
6	2	4	12
33	12	20	?

Answer to page 57

The wrapping paper costs **$.50** and the clock costs **$54.50**.

by **Terry Stickels**

Jennifer purchased a few baseball cards. All but two of the cards have a picture of a St. Louis Cardinal, all but two of the cards picture a New York Yankee, and all but two of the cards picture a Boston Red Sox player.
How many cards did Jennifer purchase?

Answer to page 58

The answer is **0**. The middle number is found by multiplying the corresponding diagonal numbers in each box and subtracting the smaller product from the larger.
Here's an example:

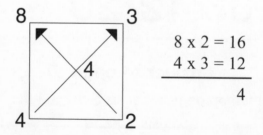

8 x 2 = 16
4 x 3 = 12
——————
4

by**Terry Stickels** [sic].

The letters around the four circles below are arranged in a logical pattern. Can you determine the pattern and figure out which letters should replace the question marks on the first circle?

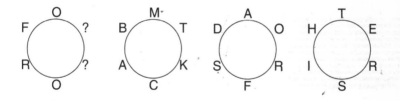

Answer to page 59

The answer is **126**. In each column, add the first two numbers, then multiply by the third number. Take that result and divide by 2 to find the bottom number in each column.

What letter should logically replace the question mark in the letter sequence below?

D H L P T ?

Answer to page 60

Jennifer purchased **3** cards.

by Terry Stickels

Below is a 3x3 grid where the center square is blacked out and not in play. Using the numbers 1 through 8 (only once each), can you place the numbers in such a fashion that no two consecutive numbers are adjacent to each other, including the short diagonals (which are marked on the grid)?

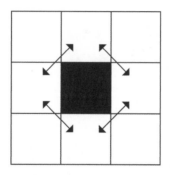

Answer to page 61

The missing letters are **N** and **T**. Starting with the **T** in the last circle, move around each circle counterclockwise, ending with the first circle. The letters spell the phrase, THIS READS FROM BACK TO FRONT.

The following seven capital letters have a feature that other capital letters don't have. Can you figure out that feature?

A B D O P Q R

Answer to page 62

The missing letter is **X**. The letter sequence represents the 4th, 8th, 12th, 16th, 20th, and 24th letters of the alphabet.

by **Terry Stickels**

I'm thinking of a number that, when added to itself, will result in an answer that is the same as if it were to be multiplied by itself. (This is not a trick; don't think of "0.") There is only one number where this is true. Can you figure out which number I'm thinking of?

Answer to page 63

3	1	4
7	■	8
5	2	6

Here's one possibility whose mirror image also would work. Can you find other possible solutions?

by**Terry Stickels**

The numbers in each of the figures below have the same relationship from figure to figure. Can you find the relationship and place the correct number in the circle with the question mark?

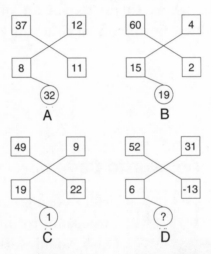

Answer to page 64

The capital letters in the puzzle are the only capital letters that contain closed-off areas in their construction.

by**Terry Stickels**

Here's a form of an old puzzle that was first seen in ancient Rome. Our friend the "Stick Dog" is facing to the left. By moving only two of the sticks, can you make him face right?

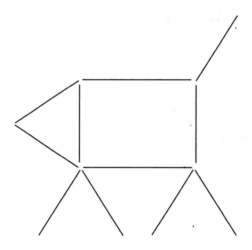

Answer to page 65

The number is **2**. It is the only number where the answer is the same whether it is added to itself or multiplied by itself.

by Terry Stickels

Of the figures below, one of them is construct-
ed in such a way that a certain feature cannot
be created within its boundaries. Can you
deduce which figure doesn't belong with the
others?

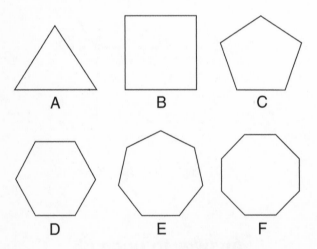

A   B   C

D   E   F

Answer to page 66

The missing number is **24**. In each of the
four figures, the five numbers add up to 100.

[sic].

by**Terry Stickels**

The seven pairs of letters below share a common pattern. Which one of the five pairs below belongs with this set?

GT JQ KP DW

CX IR HS

Choose from:

DE AY KZ LO ET

Answer to page 67

Here's how to make the "Stick Dog" face right by moving only two of the sticks.

by**Terry Stickels**

See if you can determine the logic of this number array and come up with the missing number. A little help: Number arrays can be determined vertically, horizontally, both combined and, in some cases, diagonally.

8	9	6	12
11	10	5	22
16	7	28	4
4	24	48	?

Answer to page 68

Figure **A**, the triangle, does not belong with the others. It is the only figure in which a diagonal cannot be drawn.

Below is a message written in code. Can you decipher the message?
Hint: QWERTYUIOP

O KIDY DP;BRF

YJOD [IXX;R

Answer to page 69

LO belongs with the original set. The letters are paired from the outside letters of the alphabet moving inward:
AZ, **BY**, **CX**, **DW**, etc.

71

by Terry Stickels

Can you draw the next figure in this logical sequence?

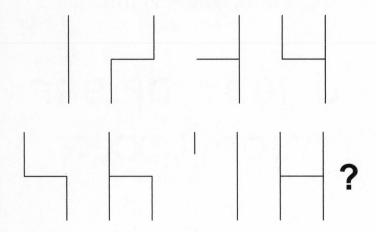

?

Answer to page 70

The missing number is **2**. The number array was a horizontal one, where the first two numbers in each row are multiplied and the result is divided by the third number. This gives you the fourth number in each row.

by Terry Stickels

Here is a magic square where the rows, columns, and diagonals each add up to 41.
No number is used more than once, and the largest number is 26. Can you fill in the missing numbers?

2			26
		5	
	1		
9			4

Answer to page 71

The puzzle should read:

I JUST SOLVED THIS PUZZLE.

Looking at the keyboard of any typewriter or computer, move one key to the left of each letter or symbol in the code.

by**Terry Stickels**

Can you figure out the two missing letters in the sequence below?

A D B E H F

I L J M ? ?

Answer to page 72

The next figure should look like this: ⌐|

The sequence is the numbers 1 through 9 with the top and bottom horizontal lines omitted from each figure.

1 2 3 4 5 6 7 8 9

by**Terry Stickels**

Can you figure out the next letter in the sequence below?

P O I U Y T R E W ?

Answer to page 73

2	6	7	26
12	21	5	3
18	1	14	8
9	13	15	4

Can you arrange the numbers 1 through 6 in such a way that any three numbers in the same line will total 12?

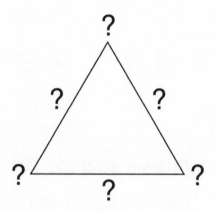

Answer to page 74

The missing letters are **P** and **N**. In order to figure out the sequence, start with the letter A, then move up three letters (D), then back two letters (B). Repeat the pattern with E, up three (H), back two (F). Then I, up three (L), back two (J). Do the same with M and get the answer.

by Terry Stickels

Can you determine the values (whole numbers) for each of the four symbols in the grid below?

★	★	□	○	15
△	□	○	★	14
△	★	★	△	18
○	□	○	★	12

15 16 12 16 18

Answer to page 75

The missing letter is **Q**. The sequence is the top row of a keyboard, backward.

A certain rock group has five members, and the group receives $30,000 per performance. The lead singer receives twice as much money as each of the four other members of the band.

How much money does the lead singer and each of the other four band members receive per performance?

Answer to page 76
Here's one way to solve this.

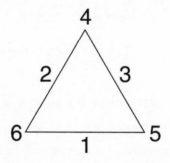

by**Terry Stickels**

Below are five names followed by a curious, but logical code. See if you can crack the code and assign the appropriate number to GUS.

KIM = 11913
ART = 11820
DEB = 452
POP = 161516
GUS = ?

Answer to page 79

The common four-letter word is: **RAIN**

Which of the six words below does not
belong with the others?

Peppermint
Horsehide
Steeplechase
Dormitory
Firehouse
Coinage

Answer to page 80

The grid forms a simple addition
problem. The missing numbers
are 8 and 8.

$$\begin{array}{r} 40,653 \\ 28,122 \\ +\ 15,763 \\ \hline 84,538 \end{array}$$

by**Terry Stickels**

What comes next in the following sequence?

EIGHT
FIVE
FOUR
NINE
ONE
SEVEN
?

Answer to page 81

GUS = 72119.
The code is: A = 1, B = 2, C = 3 ... Z = 26
(G=7, U=21, S=19)

by Terry Stickels

The nine letters in the grid below are placed in a logical sequence that spells out a word. Can you figure out what the word is?

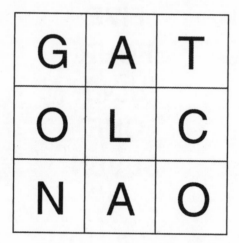

G	A	T
O	L	C
N	A	O

Answer to page 82

DORMITORY doesn't belong because it's the only word that cannot be divided to create two new words.
(i.e., PEPPERMINT: PEPPER & MINT)

 [sic].

by **Terry Stickels**

The following words share an
interesting characteristic.
Can you figure it out?
HINT: Try typing these words on a
keyboard and see what happens.

POTTERY
QUITTER
POTPOURRI
TYPEWRITER
POETRY

Answer to page 83

The next word should be **SIX**.
The list is the first seven numbers in
alphabetical order.

by Terry Stickels

The letters in the wheel below are situated in a logical way in order to spell a word. Can you figure out the word?

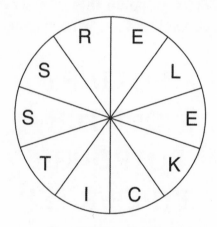

Answer to page 84

The word is **OCTAGONAL**.
Starting with the "O" in the lower right-hand corner, follow the letters counterclockwise around the outside of the square, ending with the "L" in the center.

**Fill in the missing sum of the diagonal by assigning
numbers to the letters. (Use the
lowest possible integers. Hint: X=3.)**

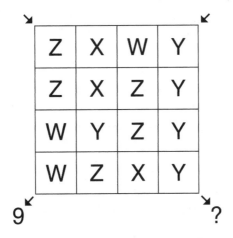

9   ?

Answer to page 85

All of the words are formed by using only the
top row of a keyboard.

by **Terry Stickels**

What should logically replace the question marks in the sequence below?

J - 30
J - 31
A - 31
S - 30
? - ?

Answer to page 86

The word is STICKELERS!
Starting with the "S," move counterclockwise to reveal the word.

by Terry Stickels

If you are a female, what is your relationship to your father's mother-in-law's only daughter's only daughter?

Answer to page 87

1	3	4	2
1	3	1	2
4	2	1	2
4	1	3	2

9   7

If you spend some time looking at the columns and rows, you see that there is a logic to them, as shown in the key below.

Z = 1
Y = 2
X = 3
W = 4

Below is an unfolded cube with the numbers 1, 2, and 4 on three of its faces. Can you place the numbers 3, 5, and 6 so that when the cube is reformed, the opposite faces will total 7?

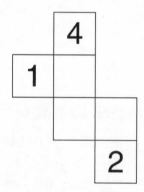

Answer to page 88

The question marks should be replaced with

O - 31

The sequence is simply the first letters of the months, starting with June, and followed by the number of days in that particular month.

 [sic].

by**Terry Stickels**

Below is a grid that has a certain logic to it. Can you determine the logic and fill in the missing number from the choices listed below the grid?

10	9	5	14
3	9	5	7
4	7	3	8
11	6	2	?

CHOICES: **0 7 12 15**

Answer to page 89

The answer is **YOU**. If you are a female, **YOU** are your father's mother-in-law's only daughter's only daughter.

by **Terry Stickels**

Five of the six words below share a common characteristic. Can you figure out which word doesn't belong with the others?

STAB
STARS
GHOST
HIGH
DESIST
EFFORT

Answer to page 90

With the numbers placed as shown in the diagram to the right, when the cube is reformed, the opposite sides will each add up to seven.

	4	
1	5	
	3	6
		2

Can you draw 2 straight lines on the figure below so that you end up with 3 identical arrows?

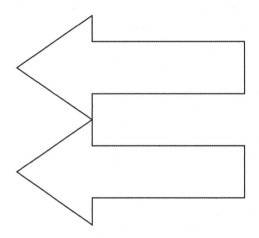

Answer to page 91

15 should replace the question mark in the grid. In each of the four rows, the sum of the first two numbers is equal to the sum of the third and fourth numbers.

by Terry Stickels

Which of the seven words below does not belong with the others?
Note: The difference has nothing to do with their meaning or part of speech.

PUNTING   NEPHEWS   DAZZLED

POSTURE   SHADOWS

DANCING   TUNNELS

Answer to page 92

EFFORT doesn't belong with the others because the other five all begin with two consecutive letters of the alphabet and end with two consecutive letters of the alphabet.

by**Terry Stickels**

The analogy below consists of several shapes. The first shape relates to the second shape as the third relates to the fourth. Which shape, from choices A, B, C, and D, completes the analogy?

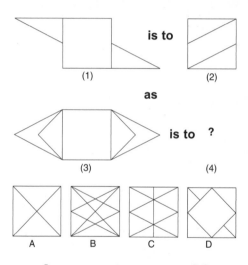

is to

(1)   (2)

as

is to   ?

(3)   (4)

A   B   C   D

Answer to page 93

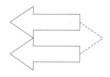

by Terry Stickels

Here's a puzzle I call a "trickle-down" puzzle. The rules are simple: You merely change one letter on each line to make a new word and continue until you reach the final word.

Example:	COAT	Answer:	COAT
	____		COST
	____		CAST
	____		CASE
	VASE		VASE

Now try this one:

JUMP

____

____

DATE

Answer to page 94

POSTURE does not belong with the others. It is the only word with three vowels; the other words all have two vowels.

Arthur, Bobbi, Cheri, and Dan are at their weekly luncheon. Their occupations are actor, botanist, carpenter, and drummer, but not necessarily in that order. Dan just told the botanist that Cheri was going to be late to the luncheon. Arthur is sitting across from the drummer and next to the carpenter. The drummer never said a word. Can you figure out the occupation of each person?

Answer to page 95

The answer is **B**. If you fold the two wing flaps from figure 1 toward the middle, you get figure 2. If you fold the flaps from figure 3 toward the middle, the result would be choice B.

Below are 10 toothpicks formed to make 3 squares. Can you move just 2 toothpicks to wind up with just 2 squares? The catch is that you cannot just remove two toothpicks; your solution must include all 10 toothpicks.

Answer to page 96

Here's one way
to solve this
trickle-down:

JUMP
DUMP
DAMP
DAME
DATE

STICKELERS [sic].

by**Terry Stickels**

The following anagram contains the title of a famous work of art. Quick! Can you unscramble the letters and name this well-known masterpiece?

HA! NOT A SMILE

Answer to page 97

Since Dan spoke to the botanist, and Arthur was sitting next to the carpenter and across from the drummer, Cheri must be the actor and Arthur, the botanist. The drummer didn't speak, but Dan did, so Bobbi is the drummer and Dan is the carpenter.

Here's another "trickle-down" puzzle. The rules are simple: You merely change one letter on each line to make a new word and continue until you reach the final word.

Now try
this one:

ZANY

———

———

———

MICE

Answer to page 98

by Terry Stickels

Below are seven words that share a common characteristic. Can you figure it out? Note: The common characteristic has nothing to do with meaning or parts of speech, and it's easier than it looks!

TRAINER
CYCLONE
PUNTING
POSTURE
DANCING
DAZZLED
NEPHEWS

Answer to page 99
THE MONA LISA

by**Terry Stickels**

How many squares of any size are in the figure below?

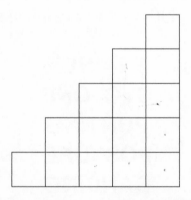

Answer to page 100

Here's one way
to solve this
trickle-down:

ZANY
MANY
MANE
MINE
MICE

byTerry Stickels

Here's a "trickle-down" puzzle. The rules are simple: You merely change one letter on each line to make a new word and continue until you reach the final word.

Try this one:

TAILOR

———

———

———

———

———

FOOTED

Answer to page 101

Each of the seven words has seven letters.

Connecting three dots at a time on the figure below to make a triangle of any size, shape, or orientation each time, what is the maximum number of triangles possible? We gave you a start by showing you 16 small equilateral triangles of the same size. Hint: Be careful with this. There may be more than you think!

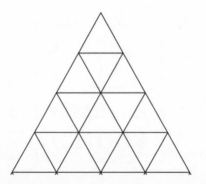

Answer to page 102

There are **22** squares.

Can you arrange the numbers 1 through 9 in the diagram below in such a way that the sum of the three numbers in any straight spoke equals 15?

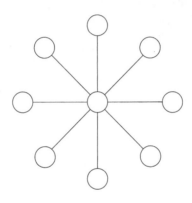

Answer to page 103

Here's one way to solve this trickle-down puzzle:

TAILOR
TAILER
TAILED
FAILED
FOILED
FOOLED
FOOTED

Mary's mother gave her a 6-gallon unmarked bucket and a 5-gallon unmarked bucket. She instructed Mary to take the two buckets to the river and bring back exactly 9 gallons of water. How did Mary accomplish this?

Answer to page 104
There are **407** triangles.

All of the letters below, except one, share a common characteristic. Can you figure out which letter doesn't belong with the others?
Hint: Disregard the fact that the "O" is the only closed figure.

H I J N O S X Z

Answer to page 105

The number 5 must always be in the center of the wheel. Here's one solution:

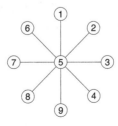

Five of the six figures below share a common characteristic. Can you figure out which figure does not belong with the others?

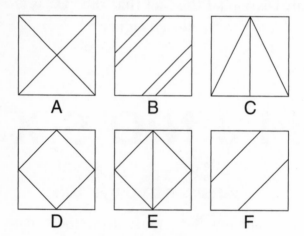

A   B   C

D   E   F

Answer to page 106

1) Fill the 5-gallon bucket and dump it into the 6-gallon bucket.
2) Fill up the 5-gallon bucket again and fill the remainder of the 6-gallon bucket, leaving 4 gallons in the 5-gallon bucket.
3) Dump the 6-gallon bucket and put the 4 gallons from the 5-gallon bucket into the 6-gallon bucket.
4) Now refill the 5-gallon bucket for a total of 9 gallons.

STICKELERS [sic].
by Terry Stickels

Each of the "cars" below follow the same rules to come up with the number in the middle. Can you figure out the missing number in the last car?

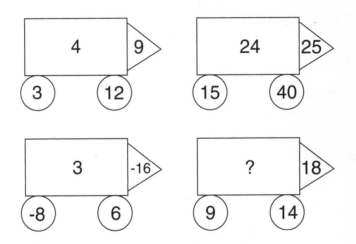

Answer to page 107

The letter **J** does not belong with the others. All of the other letters will appear the same when flipped upside down.

I have a bag of gumdrops that contains 500 candies in 5 different colors. The gumdrops are evenly divided so there are 100 of each color. If you are blindfolded, what is the least number of gumdrops that must be picked before you can be sure there are 5 gumdrops of the same color?

Answer to page 108

Figure **C** doesn't belong with the others. It is the only figure that contains an odd number of triangles.

Here's a fun puzzle that can be solved
quickly if you grasp that "Aha!" moment:
Six dollars are exchanged for nickels and dimes.
The number of nickels was the same as the
number of dimes. Quick now, how many nickels
were in the change?

Answer to page 109

The missing number is **7**. Multiply the wheels
of each car, then divide by the triangular nose
to arrive at the number in the middle.

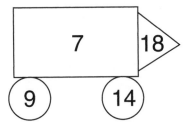

The 12 letters in the grid below are strung together in a logical way to spell a word. Can you figure out the word?

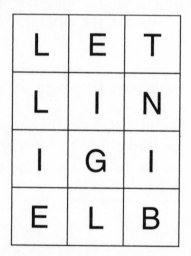

Answer to page 110

You would need to pick **21** gumdrops to be sure you had 5 of the same color.

Which of the five figures below cannot be folded into an octahedron?

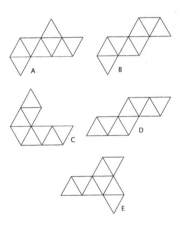

Answer to page 111

There were **40** nickels ($2) and **40** dimes ($4) for a total of $6. Since it takes two nickels to have the same value as one dime, you will always have twice the value of dimes if you have the same number of each coin.

[sic].

by Terry Stickels

Here's a "trickle-down" puzzle. The rules are simple: You merely change one letter on each line to make a new word and continue until you reach the final word.

Try this one:

> **BALD**
>
> ———
>
> ———
>
> ———
>
> **TIRE**

Answer to page 112

Follow the numbered boxes to reveal the hidden word, **INTELLIGIBLE**.

L₅	E₄	T₃
L₆	I₁	N₂
I₇	G₈	I₉
E₁₂	L₁₁	B₁₀

Can you figure out the analogy below?

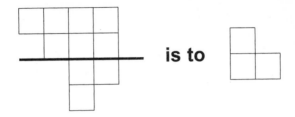

is to

as

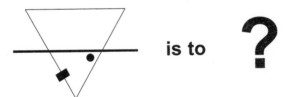

is to   **?**

Answer to page 113

Figure **C** does not belong with the others.
No correctly unfolded octahedron can have
five triangles around one point.

STICKELERS [sic].

by **Terry Stickels**

Below are some names of people that share an interesting common characteristic. See if you can guess what it is and complete the puzzle.

If I choose Leona Noel, N.Y. Llewellyn, and Edna Lalande to play on a puzzle team, what would my next pick most likely be?

N.A. Gahagan
or
R.J. Kroker, Jr.

Answer to page 114

Here's one way to solve
this trickle-down puzzle:

BALD
BALE
TALE
TILE
TIRE

by Terry Stickels

Can you figure out what is so unusual
about the sentence below?

"I DO NOT KNOW WHERE FAMILY DOCTORS ACQUIRED ILLEGIBLY PERPLEXING HANDWRITING"

*Special thanks to Martin Gardner for
his help with this puzzle.

Answer to page 115
The missing figure is the figure below
the line, rotated 90 degrees.

**Which word below doesn't belong
with the others?**

SISTER
COUSIN
FATHER
AUNT
MOTHER
UNCLE
BROTHER

Answer to page 116

You would probaly pick **N.A. Gahagan**.
It's similar to the other names in that each
is a palindrome. That is, the names read the
same forward as they do backward.

Here's a "trickle-down" puzzle. The rules are simple: You merely change one letter on each line to make a new word and continue until you reach the final word.

Try this one:

THINK

_____

_____

_____

_____

START

Answer to page 117

In this sentence, each successive word contains one more letter than the preceding word.

If box #1 fits inside box #2 and box #3 fits inside box #4 and boxes #4 and #1 are the same size, then which of the following statements must be true?

1) BOX #1 FITS INSIDE BOX #4

2) BOX #2 CANNOT FIT INSIDE BOX #3

3) BOX #4 CANNOT FIT INSIDE BOX #2

4) BOX #3 CANNOT FIT INSIDE BOX #1

Answer to page 118

The word **Cousin** does not belong because it doesn't specify male or female the way the others do.

by**Terry Stickels**

Below is a figure that represents a 5-inch-by-5-inch square, along with a circle with a diameter of 1 inch. What is the maximum number of circles that can be packed into the square?

Answer to page 119

Here's one way to solve this trickle-down puzzle:

THINK
THANK
SHANK
SHARK
STARK
START

by Terry Stickels

Here's some analogy fun. No tricks or gimmicks — just pick the correct answer from the choices given.

1) HOUR : MINUTE : : MINUTE : ?
a) day b) week c) second d) time

2) H : 8 : : X : ?
a) 30 b) 10 c) 24 d) 1

3) PART : LOOP : : TRAP : ?
a) puzzle b) loops c) smile d) pool

4) I : WE : : MOOSE : ?
a) mouse b) moose c) mooses d) no answer

Answer to page 120

Statement **2** is correct,
BOX #2 CANNOT FIT INSIDE BOX #3.

STICKELERS [sic].
by**Terry Stickels**

How many triangles of any size are in the figure below?

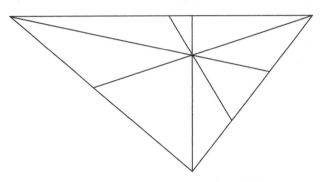

Answer to page 121

You can fit **27** 1-inch diameter circles inside a 5-inch-by-5-inch square.

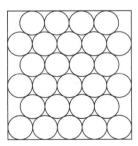

What should the next arrangement of circle, triangle, and square logically be in the figure below?

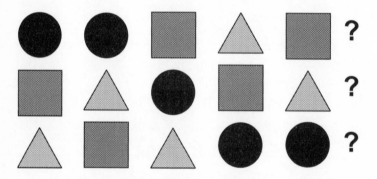

Answer to page 122

1) **c - second**—60 minutes in an hour; 60 seconds in a minute
2) **c - 24**—H is the 8th letter of the alphabet, and X is the 24th
3) **d - pool**—these are words spelled forward and backward
4) **b - moose**—singular to plural

One of the following quadrilaterals does not belong with the others. Can you figure out which one, and why? Hint: It has to do with a simple, basic straightforward design feature.

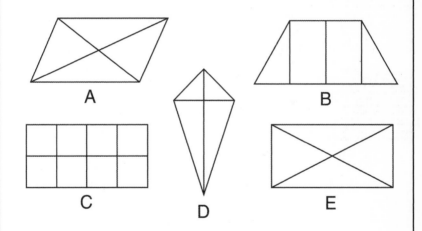

Answer to page 123

There are **23** triangles.

by **Terry Stickels**

Can you draw the figure that should go in the
question-marked box in order to logically
complete the grid below?

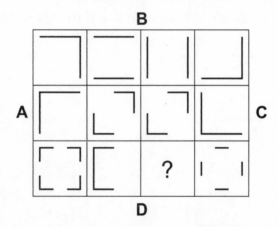

Answer to page 124

This is the only combination
of circle, triangle,
and square that did not
appear in the figure.

126

by Terry Stickels

Find the letter that comes below the letter that comes after K and the letter that comes above the letter T and diagonal from J.

A	B	C	D	E
F	G	H	I	J
K	L	M	N	O
P	R	S	T	U
V	W	X	Y	Z

Answer to page 125

Figure **A** does not belong with the others because it is the only figure that doesn't contain a 90-degree angle.

In a foreign language, LOF ATRIB RALK means *eat green grapes*. TPIR RALK NARP means *big green bugs*. ATRIBO ATRIB RALK means *often green grapes*. How do you say *eat bugs often?*

Answer to page 126

This is the shape that should fill the empty spot on the grid:

If you fold point **A** to point **C** along the **BD** axis, each of the separate boxes will form a perfect square.

Can you determine which figure
does not belong with the others in
the diagram below?

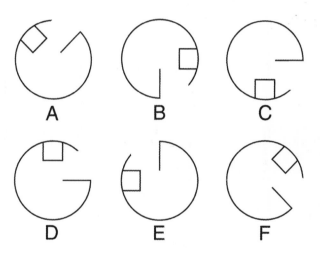

A   B   C

D   E   F

Answer to page 127

The mystery letter is **S**.

**Which word below does not belong
with the others?**

GOUT   KNOB   HOUR

PSALM   GNOME   EUCHRE

Answer to page 128

ATRIBO LOF TPIR
means *eat bugs often.*

What four-letter word can be placed in front of the five words below to form five new words.

WRECK

YARD

MATE

BUILDER

SHAPE

Answer to page 129

Figure **C** does not belong with the others. All of the other figures form the letter G, whereas figure C forms a backward G.

by Terry Stickels

Below is a 10 x10 grid that contains the name of a former country that happens to have 10 letters. Can you find the 10-letter country?

R	O	M	P	Z	Q	T	A	B	Y
E	M	S	A	N	A	R	C	U	A
E	A	L	R	I	T	A	G	L	L
R	Z	O	A	R	A	O	R	G	T
G	E	I	G	Y	S	C	E	A	E
L	L	J	U	L	P	S	E	R	R
O	W	L	A	T	A	C	C	I	S
G	G	V	O	Y	I	J	D	O	L
N	I	L	F	X	R	U	V	B	N
A	N	T	A	R	C	T	I	Z	O

Answer to page 130

If you said **GOUT** doesn't belong, you'd be correct because it is the only word that doesn't begin with a silent letter. **EUCHRE** would also be correct because it is the only word that starts with a vowel and ends in one too.

by**Terry Stickels**

How many triangles of any size are in the figure below?

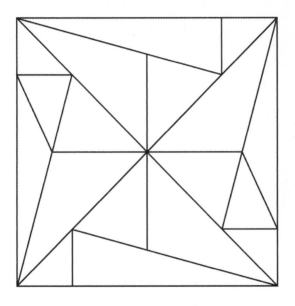

Answer to page 131

If you add the word **SHIP** to the beginning of the words, they form five more common words.

by **Terry Stickels**

Here's a "trickle-down" puzzle. The rules are simple: You merely change one letter on each line to make a new word and continue until you reach the final word.

Try this one:

CHILL

——————

——————

——————

——————

STARE

Answer to page 132

At the end of the first row is a Y, the first letter in YUGOSLAVIA. It runs from the upper right-hand corner of the grid to the lower left.

Can you change the position of two of the lines below to make four squares, all of the same size with no lines left over?

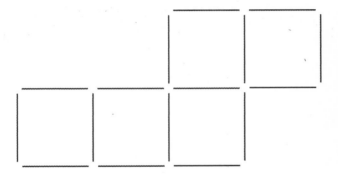

Answer to page 133

There are **38** triangles.

One of the five words below does not belong with the others. Which one is the odd man out?

NOMINATED

SOMETIMES

RATED

RADICAL

GUMDROP

Answer to page 134

Here's one way to solve this trickle-down puzzle:

CHILL
SHILL
SHALL
STALL
STALE
STARE

Which of the six letters below does
not belong with the others?

g b j
p q y

Answer to page 135

	new	X	
new			
	X		

Four of the five words below share an interesting characteristic. Can you figure out which word doesn't belong with the others?

HIJACK

BILATERAL

COUGHING

THIRSTY

DEFIANT

Answer to page 136

GUMDROP does not belong with the others. The other four words alternate vowel-consonant-vowel-consonant, etc.

Here's a "trickle-down" puzzle. The rules are simple: You merely change one letter on each line to make a new word and continue until you reach the final word.

Try this one:

> PARTY
>
> _____
>
> _____
>
> _____
>
> _____
>
> DINES

Answer to page 137

The letter **b** does not belong with the others. The other letters all have "tails" that would hang below a written line.

by Terry Stickels

There is a logical pattern to the letters in the boxes below that spells out a short phrase. Can you determine the pattern and replace the question mark with the appropriate letter?

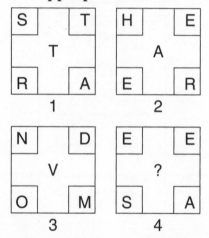

S		T
	T	
R		A

1

H		E
	A	
E		R

2

N		D
	V	
O		M

3

E		E
	?	
S		A

4

Answer to page 138

BILATERAL does not belong with the others. The other four words contain three consecutive letters of the alphabet:
HIJACK, COUGHING, THIRSTY, DEFIANT

Five of the six words below share a common characteristic. Can you figure out which word does not belong?

PUTTER
GRIPE
SOUGHT
CLEAN
GHOST
RUNNER

Answer to page 139

Here's one way to solve this trickle-down puzzle:	PARTY
	PARTS
	PANTS
	PINTS
	PINES
	DINES

Using the numbers remaining from 1 through 16, can you fill in the blank squares so that the sum of each row, column, and diagonal each produce the same sum?

16	15	1	2
	10		
9	6	12	7

Answer to page 140

The missing letter is **T**. Starting with the first box and moving clockwise, you'll notice it spells the word **START**; following the same pattern in the following boxes, the phrase is: **START HERE AND MOVE EAST**

by**Terry Stickels**

The cube on the right unfolds into one of the flattened representations below, can you figure out which one?

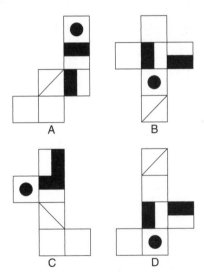

A   B

C   D

Answer to page 141

RUNNER does not belong with the others.
If you remove the first letter from the other five
words, they each form a new word.

Below are three anagram phrases. Each is the name of a state. Can you figure out the name of each state?

1) SADDLE RHINO

2) ASSESS MATH CUT

3) IF OIL, AN ARC

Answer to page 142

16	15	1	2
4	3	13	14
5	10	8	11
9	6	12	7

by**Terry Stickels**

There is a logical sequence in the set of numbers below. Can you figure out what number should come next?

9 21 51 81 12 42 ?

Answer to page 143

Figure **B** can be folded into the cube shown in yesterday's puzzle.

by Terry Stickels

Assuming all rows and columns run to completion
unless you actually see them end, how many cubes
are in the three-dimensional figure below?

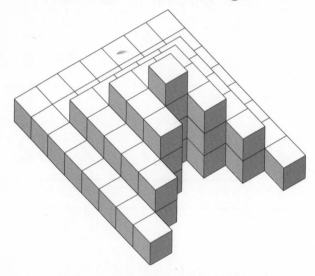

Answer to page 144

1) RHODE ISLAND
2) MASSACHUSETTS
3) CALIFORNIA

Below are five different views of one cube and one view of another cube. Can you determine which cube is the odd man out?

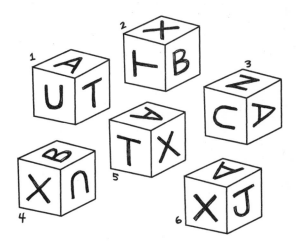

Answer to page 145

The number **72** should come next in the sequence. Each number increases by three, (for example: 9, 12, 15, 18, 21, 24), and then the double-digit numbers are reversed.

by**Terry Stickels**

There is an old alphametic puzzle that looks like this:

ONE

TWO

+ FOUR

SEVEN

Each letter has a different number value that makes the addition correct. There are eight solutions to this puzzle, but only one where W = 8. can you figure this one out?

Answer to page 146

77 total cubes.

The cube on the right unfolds into one of the flattened representations below. Can you figure out which one?

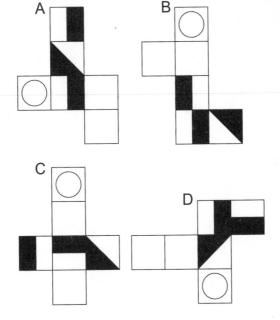

A

B

C

D

Answer to page 147

Cube **4** does not belong with the others.

STICKELERS [sic].

by**Terry Stickels**

Assuming all rows and columns run to completion unless you actually see them end, how many cubes are in the three-dimensional figure below?

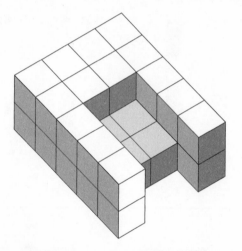

Answer to page 148

$$
\begin{array}{r}
350 \\
683 \\
+\ 9372 \\
\hline
10405
\end{array}
$$

by**Terry Stickels**

Below are three "squeezer" puzzles. Can you insert a word between each pair of given words to create two new words? The blanks between each pair indicate how many letters are in the missing word.

RUN   _ _ _   WARD

SPRING   _ _ _ _ _   WALK

SEA   _ _ _ _ _   MELON

Answer to page 149

Figure **B** represents the unfolded cube.

A phrase is hidden in the sequence below. Can you figure out the phrase and the missing letter in the last figure?

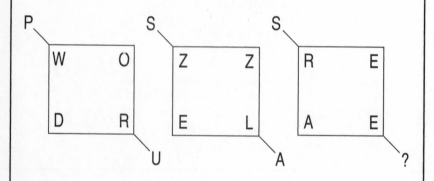

P
W   O
D   R
U

S
Z   Z
E   L
A

S
R   E
A   E
?

Answer to page 150

32 total cubes.

by Terry Stickels

Which of the five words below does not belong with the others?

ENTRAPMENT

ENTREPRENEUR

ENTERTAINMENT

ENTANGLEMENT

ENTICEMENT

Answer to page 151

RUN**WAY**WARD

SPRING**BOARD**WALK

SEA**WATER**MELON

byTerry Stickels

Can you determine the logic in the figures below and fill in the missing numbers in the last figure?

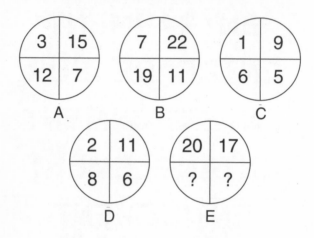

Answer to page 152

The missing letter is **Y**. Starting with the **W** inside the first square and following the letters clockwise to the **P** and the **U** outside the square, continue to the next figure following the same pattern, and you'll find the mystery phrase:

WORD PUZZLES ARE EASY

by**Terry Stickels**

Below is a magic square. Once complete, all rows, columns, and diagonals add up to the same sum. Can you fill in the missing numbers?

3	16			15
	8	21	14	
	25			19
24		5	18	
11			10	23

Answer to page 153

ENTREPRENEUR does not belong with the others. All of the other words start with **ENT** and end with **ENT**.

Can you figure out what number should come next in the sequence below?

1   4   10   22   46   94   ?

Answer to page 154

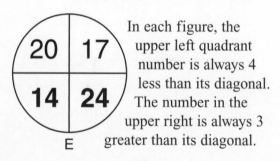

In each figure, the upper left quadrant number is always 4 less than its diagonal. The number in the upper right is always 3 greater than its diagonal.

156

Which of the five words below does not belong with the others?

PSYCHE

AISLE

HONESTY

FENCE

KNOWLEDGE

Answer to page 155

3	16	9	22	15
20	8	21	14	2
7	25	13	1	19
24	12	5	18	6
11	4	17	10	23

by **Terry Stickels**

Can you figure out what the missing number in the last box should be?

8	6
12	11

7	1
3	26

15	13
5	4

9	2
10	16

14	0
16	?

Answer to page 156

The missing number is **190**.
The difference between each succeeding number
is as follows:
3, 6, 12, 24, 48, 96

Can you determine the logic of each figure to arrive at the missing number in the last figure?

7		6		5		8		13		15
25				5				12		
2		1		4		3		9		12

21		27		30		19
	30				?	
16		21		21		14

Answer to page 157

FENCE does not belong with the others. The other four words all begin with a silent letter.

Below are three different views of
the same cube. What letter is on the
face opposite H?

Answer to page 158

The missing number is 7.
The sum of the four numbers
in each box is 37.

by**Terry Stickels**

I've removed the vowels from the following five countries. Can you figure out what the countries are?

1) CND
2) SRL
3) STRL
4) RGNTN
5) GRC

Answer to page 159

30		19
	45	
21		14

The missing number is **45**. To arrive at this number, you must first find the difference between the upper and lower numbers on the left-hand side (9), then find the difference between the upper and lower numbers on the righthand side (5), then multiply the two numbers (45).

by**Terry Stickels**

Can you determine the missing number in figure F?

12	30	4
15	6	45
A	B	C

36	20	3
5	9	?
D	E	F

Answer to page 160

S is on the face opposite **H**.
S is used twice.

Hidden in the grid below is the first and
last name of someone famous. Can you
find the name?

O	R	A	I
B	J	U	L
E	R	T	S

Answer to page 161

1) CND = CANADA
2) SRL = ISRAEL
3) STRL = AUSTRALIA
4) RGNTN = ARGENTINA
5) GRC = GREECE

 [sic].

by Terry Stickels

Here's a "trickle-down" puzzle. The rules are simple: You change one letter on each line to make a new word and continue until you reach the final word.

Try this one:

GLOOM

———

———

———

———

BREAD

Answer to page 162

The missing number is **60**.
The product of each pair is 180.

by **Terry Stickels** [sic].

Quickly now, can you think of
at least one word that begins with ER
and ends with ER?

Answer to page 163

JULIA ROBERTS

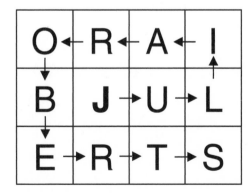

by Terry Stickels

Which figure matches this cube once it has been unfolded?

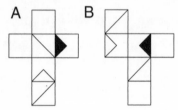

A   B

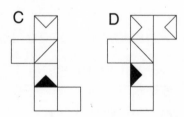

C   D

Answer to page 164

Here's one way
to solve this
trickle-down:

GLOOM
BLOOM
BROOM
BROOD
BROAD
BREAD

by**Terry Stickels**

Can you figure out the missing letter in triangle 5?

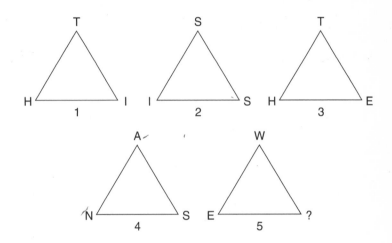

Answer to page 165

ERASER begins with ER and ends with ER. Did you think of others?

What letter can be placed in the middle of the figure below so that, when it is added to the scrambled letters, each one of the four sections forms four different words?

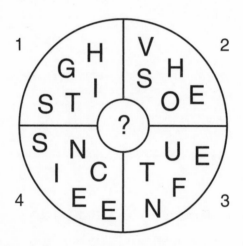

Answer to page 166

Choice **A** represents the unfolded cube.

Can you determine the missing number in figure E?

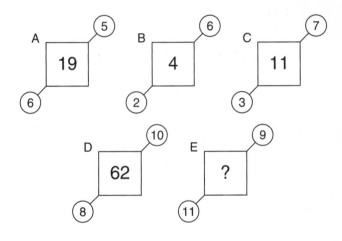

Answer to page 167

The missing letter is **R**.
If you start at the top and follow the letters counterclockwise around each triangle, from one to the next, it forms the phrase:

THIS IS THE ANSWER

by Terry Stickels

**Which one of the five words below
is spelled incorrectly?**

MILIEU

COMMITMENT

OCCASION

SILHOUETTE

CONCILLIATION

Answer to page 168

The letter in the middle should be L.
1) LIGHTS
2) SHOVEL
3) FLUENT
4) SILENCE

The same five letter word can be placed either in front of or behind each of the words below to form four new words. Can you determine the five letter word's identity?

KEY

WALL

GEM

WASHED

– – – – –

Answer to page 169

The missing number is **79**.
In each figure multiply the two circled numbers, then subtract the sum of the two circled numbers from that number to arrive at the boxed number.

by**Terry Stickels**

Here's a "trickle-down" puzzle. The rules are simple: You change one letter on each line to make a new word and continue until you reach the final word.

Try this one:

CREST

——————

——————

——————

——————

SHOWS

Answer to page 170

CONCILLIATION is spelled incorrectly. It should be spelled **CONCILIATION**.

Can you determine the logic behind the figures below to find the missing number in figure D?

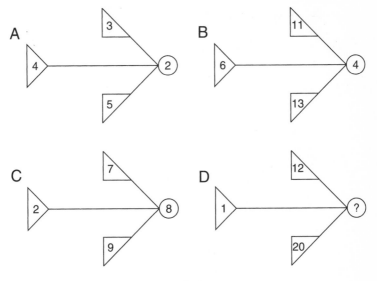

Answer to page 171

The key word is **STONE**.

keySTONE

STONEwall

gemSTONE

STONEwall

Using any math symbols you like,
can you make four **8**s equal **2**?

8 8 8 8

Answer to page 172

Here's one way
to solve this
trickle-down:

CREST
CHEST
CHESS
CHEWS
CHOWS
SHOWS

by**Terry Stickels**

**Below is a letter square with the letter Q
missing that makes a 5-by-5 square.
Now here's the puzzle: Find the letter that comes
just above the letter which comes between the
letter just before the letter just below G and the
letter just before the letter just above T.**

A	B	C	D	E
F	G	H	I	J
K	L	M	N	O
P	R	S	T	U
V	W	X	Y	Z

Answer to page 173

The missing number is **32**.
First add the two wing numbers, then
divide that number by the tail number to
arrive at the circled number.

It's rare when a word has two anagrams, even more rare is when it has three, and extremely rare when it contains more than that.

Using the letters below, how many different words can you create?

E N T L S I

Answer to page 174

Here's one way to solve this math problem:

8/8 + 8/8 = 1+1 or 2

STICKELERS [sic].

by**Terry Stickels**

Assuming all rows and columns run to completion unless you actually see them end, how many individual cubes are in the diagram below?

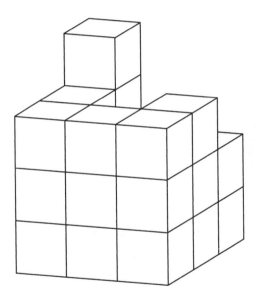

Answer to page 175

The mystery letter is **G**.

Below are six sticks of the same size.
What is the maximum number of
triangles of any size that can be
created from these six sticks?

Answer to page 176

ENLIST
INLETS
LISTEN
SILENT
TINSEL

by Terry Stickels

Below is an unfolded cube that can be put together to form one of the five cubes below it. Can you figure out which of the five is the correct one?

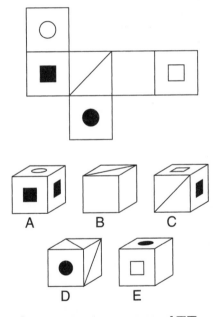

A B C

D E

Answer to page 177

There are **25** individual cubes.

Which one of the five words below does
not belong with the others, and why?

SERIES

SPY

REPLAY

PARTY

SORTIE

Answer to page 178

Here's one way to make **8** triangles.

by**Terry Stickels**

Below are two triangles made of pennies. What is the smallest number of pennies that must be moved to transform the formation on the left to the formation on the right?

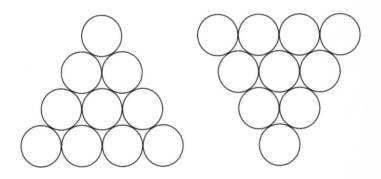

Answer to page 179

The correct cube is **E**.

by **Terry Stickels**

Can you think of at least one five letter word that ends with a Y *and* does not contain

A, E, I, O, or **U?**

Answer to page 180

REPLAY does not belong with the others. The plural of each of the others words ends in "ies", whereas the plural of REPLAY is REPLAYS.

by**Terry Stickels**

Can you come up with a word that contains at least four Fs? Oh, by the way, the word should be less than 9 letters long.

Answer to page 181

You can transform one triangle to the other by moving **3** pennies, as seen in the diagram below.

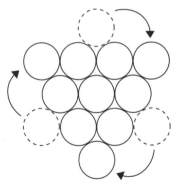

How many anagrams can you find
for the word "least"?

L E A S T

Answer to page 182

Here are two words that
satisfy this puzzle:
PYGMY and **GYPSY**

by**Terry Stickels**

[sic].

Here's a "trickle-down" puzzle. The rules are simple: You change one letter on each line to make a new word and continue until you reach the final word.

Try this one:

STARE

————

————

————

————

PHONY

Answer to page 183

One word is **RIFFRAFF**.
Were you able to find others?

Below are five views of the same cube.
What shape should be opposite the front
face of the fifth cube?

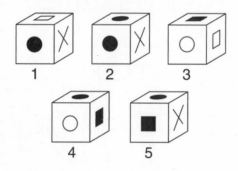

1   2   3

4   5

Answer to page 184

We found **9** anagrams.
Did you find more?
STALE, SETAL, STELA, TALES, TESLA,
SLATE, STEAL, TAELS, TEALS

by Terry Stickels

Below are three views of the same cube.
Can you figure out what letter is opposite A?
Also, what letter is opposite Y?

Answer to page 185

Here's one way
to solve this
trickle-down
puzzle:

STARE
SHARE
SHORE
SHONE
PHONE
PHONY

by **Terry Stickels**

What number should replace the question mark in the sequence below?

1 2 2 4 3 6 4 8 5 10 6 ?

Answer to page 186

A blackened circle would be opposite the front face of the fifth cube. Here is a diagram of the cube unfolded:

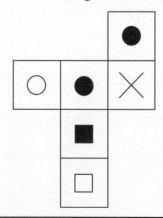

by Terry Stickels

Below are nine dots. See how many dots you can connect together without lifting your pencil where:
1) No right angles can be formed by any two lines.
2) Each line is constituted by connecting two dots.
3) No lines may intersect; however, you may draw lines through a dot more than once.

●　　　●　　　●

●　　　●　　　●

●　　　●　　　●

Answer to page 187

X is opposite **A**
N is opposite **Y**

The letters below all share a common characteristic. The question mark represents the one remaining letter that also shares this characteristic.

Can you figure out what the missing letter is?

A H I ? O T U V W X Y

Answer to page 188

This sequence is actually two sequences in one. Starting with the number 1 and reading every other number, you have the sequence 1, 2, 3, 4, 5, 6. The second sequence starts with the first 2 and proceeds 2, 4, 6, 8, 10 and **12**.

Can you figure out the logical pattern of the letters in the grid below to find the hidden word?

G	O	T	S
I	L	H	E
S	O	E	N
T	I	S	A

Answer to page 189

Here's one way to solve this puzzle with **9** lines. Can you find a way to use 10?

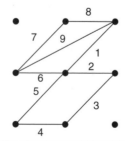

by Terry Stickels

**Can you figure out what
number should logically
replace the question mark
in figure C?**

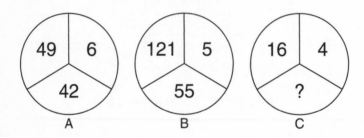

A   B   C

Answer to page 190

The missing letter is **M**.
All of the letters in this puzzle appear
the same as a mirror image.

by **Terry Stickels** [sic].

Below are three words or phrases whose letters can be reshuffled into new words or phrases that are described by them.

Here's an example:
MOON STARER = ASTRONOMER

Can you solve these three?

DIRTY ROOM = ?
FIR CONES = ?
VOICES RANT ON = ?

Answer to page 191

Starting with the **A** in the lower right-hand corner and zigzagging backward, you will find the word:

ANESTHESIOLOGIST

What figure should replace the question mark in the grid below?

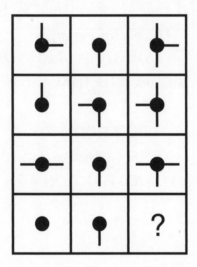

Answer to page 192

The missing number is **16**.
The answer is found by dividing the number on the
bottom by the number on the right and then squaring
the result to find the number on the left.

by Terry Stickels

Here's a "trickle-down" puzzle. The rules are simple: You change one letter on each line to make a new word and continue until you reach the final word.

Try this one:

CLASP

_____

_____

_____

_____

GROWS

Answer to page 193

DIRTY ROOM = DORMITORY
FIR CONES = CONIFERS
VOICES RANT ON = CONVERSATION

Can you determine what number should replace the missing number in figure D?

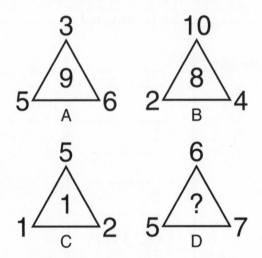

3
9
5 ⟋⟍ 6
A

10
8
2 ⟋⟍ 4
B

5
1
1 ⟋⟍ 2
C

6
?
5 ⟋⟍ 7
D

Answer to page 194

The missing figure should look like this:

The logic is to take the first two figures in each row and merge them to find the third.

STICKELERS [sic].

by **Terry Stickels**

Below are four different views of the same cube. Can you unravel the cube and place the correct faces in the squares provided to the right?

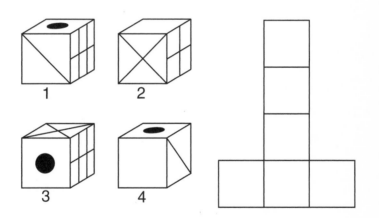

1

2

3

4

Answer to page 195

Here's one way to solve this trickle-down puzzle:

CLASP
CLASS
GLASS
GRASS
GROSS
GROWS

**LEADER is an interesting word because it
has more than one anagram.
How many can you find?**

L E A D E R

Answer to page 196

The missing number is **21**.
Multiply the outside numbers in each triangle and divide
the answer by 10 to find the number in the middle.

by**Terry Stickels**

Can you figure out the logic of the letters in the grid below to find the hidden word?
Bonus: Once you've figured out the hidden word, can you find an anagram for that word?

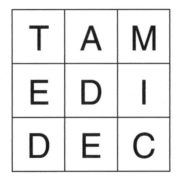

Answer to page 197

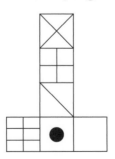

Can you determine the missing number in figure E?

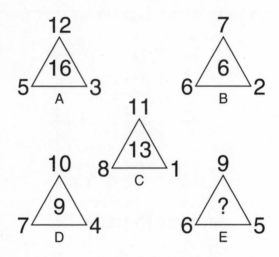

Answer to page 198
LEADER
DEALER
REDEAL
RELEAD

by**Terry Stickels**

Which of the words below does not belong with the others?

HESITATE

CAMERA

TOLERATE

COMMERCIAL

COMIC

REMOTE

Answer to page 199

Starting with the "D" in the middle of the grid, go down and then counterclockwise to find the hidden word, **DECIMATED**.

Bonus: An anagram of DECIMATED is **MEDICATED**.

**Which of the expressions below
has the greatest value?**

a) 0.06 x 2

b) 0.06 x 6

c) $\dfrac{2}{0.06}$

d) $\dfrac{0.06}{2}$

e) $\dfrac{6}{0.02}$

Answer to page 200

The missing number is 7.
Separately subtract the bottom two numbers in
each triangle from the top number, then add the
two differences to find the middle number.

by**Terry Stickels**

**Would the letter "X" go above or below
the line in the diagram below?**

A F H I K N
L T V

Answer to page 201

COMMERCIAL does not belong with the
others because all of the other words alternate
consonant, vowel, consonant, vowel, etc.

by Terry Stickels

Can you match the measuring devices to the things they measure?

1. **Chronometer**   a. Density of gas
2. **Ammeter**   b. Distance of objects
3. **Dasymeter**   c. Distances on a map
4. **Hyetometer**   d. Time
5. **Macrometer**   e. Rainfall
6. **Opisometer**   f. Electric currents

Answer to page 202
Choice **E** has the greatest value.

 [sic].

by**Terry Stickels**

See if you can figure this one out...

Robert took a test of 20 questions. The test was graded by giving 10 points for each correct answer and deducting five points for each incorrect answer. Robert answered all 20 questions and received a score of 125. How many wrong answers did he have?

Answer to page 203

The letter "X" would go below the line. The letters below the line are all created with **2** straight, different lines.

by Terry Stickels

Can you determine the missing number in the fifth figure below?

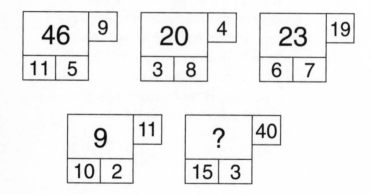

Answer to page 204

1.-d, 2.-f, 3.-a, 4.-e, 5.-b, 6.-c

by Terry Stickels

Here's a thinker ...

**Martha can row her boat
2 miles downstream in
20 minutes. She can row
her boat 2 miles upstream
in 1 hour and 20 minutes.
Can you determine the
speed of the current?**

Answer to page 205

He had five wrong answers. If Robert had answered all 20 questions correctly, he would have scored 200. Since he scored 125, this means he lost 75 points. We must deduct 15 points for each wrong answer: 10 points out of 200 that he didn't earn, plus 5 points deducted for the wrong answer. 75 divided by 15 equals 5.

by**Terry Stickels**

Do you know the plural version of each of the words below?

HANDFUL

BROTHER-IN-LAW

ROOF

CRISIS

BASS (the fish)

Answer to page 206

The missing number is **5**.
Multiply the two bottom boxes, then subtract the box to the right to find the number in the large box.

Can you determine the missing number in the last figure below?

33	12	7
46	67	72

60	-4	9
19	83	?

Answer to page 207

Going downstream, Martha can cover 6 miles in 60 minutes. Upstream, Martha can cover 1.5 miles in 60 minutes. Rowing speed is determined by adding 6 miles to 1.5 miles and dividing by 2 hours, so Martha is actually rowing an average of 3.75 miles per hour. The speed of the current is 6 mph minus 3.75 mph, which is 2.25 mph, the speed of the current.

by**Terry Stickels**

Which one of the words below does not belong with the others?

LADLE
SKILLET
SUITCASE
TABLE
HAIRBRUSH
PAIL

Answer to page 208

HANDFULS or HANDSFUL
BROTHERS-IN-LAW
ROOFS
CRISES
BASS or BASSES

Can you determine the values of the symbols in the
grid below in order to find the missing numbers
along the side of the grid?

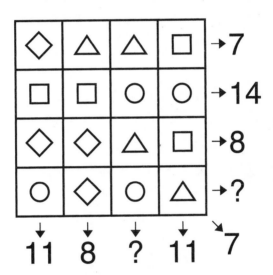

Answer to page 209

The missing number is **70**. The total of the two
numbers in each of the paired boxes is 79.

The grid below contains nine letters of a 10-letter word. Can you determine the letter that should be added to the beginning of the word in order to form the word?

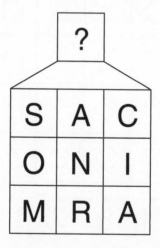

Answer to page 210

TABLE does not belong with the others.
All of the other objects have handles!

by**Terry Stickels**

Can you arrange seven toothpicks in
such a way as to create three triangles?
Keep in mind: no breaking, bending,
stacking, or any other manipulation that
does not include the seven toothpicks.

Answer to page 211

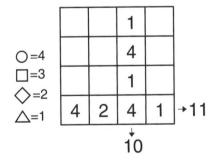

○ =4
□ =3
◇ =2
△ =1

		1	
		4	
		1	
4	2	4	1	→11

↓
10

Kelsey is standing in a line with other students. She is fifth in line counting from one end and 12th in line counting from the other end. How many students total are in the line?

Answer to page 212

The missing letter is **H**. If you add H to the A in the lower right-hand corner, then zigzag up, you'll spell **HARMONICAS**.

by Terry Stickels

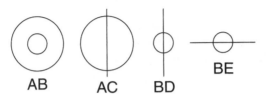

AB   AC   BD   BE

Given the four figures above, which of the four figures below most likely represents DE?

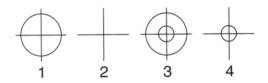

1   2   3   4

Answer to page 213

Here's one way to create three triangles using seven toothpicks. Did you find another?

215

Molly buys a beautiful necklace for $200.
Soon after, she sells it to Eleanor for $210.
Some time later, she realizes that she could
have made more money selling the
necklace, so she buys it back from Eleanor
for $220 and sells it to Meredith for $230.

What was the end result of Molly's
transactions? How much money
did she make or lose?

Answer to page 214

There are **16** students in the line.

○○○○●○○○○○○○○○○○

Fifth and 12th in line.

**Which of the following words does
not belong with the others?**

DEVILISH

SORORITY

GHASTLY

HIGHLIGHT

TURKEY

Answer to page 215

Figure **2** is the correct choice.

How many squares of any size are
in the figure below?

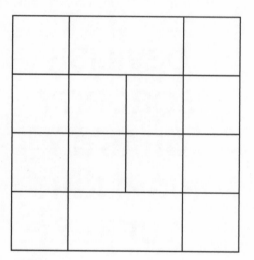

Answer to page 216

Molly made **$20**.

by**Terry Stickels**

Below is an unfolded cube.
If the figure were to be folded back
into cube form, which face would be
opposite B?

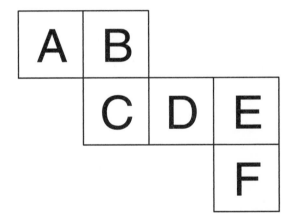

Answer to page 217

SORORITY does not belong with the others.
All of the other words start with two
consecutive letters of the alphabet.

by **Terry Stickels**

Each row in the figure below uses
the same logic to determine each
successive number. Can you figure
out what the missing number is?

2	5	11
3	10	31
4	17	?

Answer to page 218

22 squares.

by**Terry Stickels**

See if you can figure this one out ...

100 students are majoring
in math, business or both.
72% of the students are
business majors, and 58%
are math majors.
How many students
are majoring in both?

Answer to page 219

F would be the face opposite B.

**How many different pairs of parallel lines
are in a normal cube?**

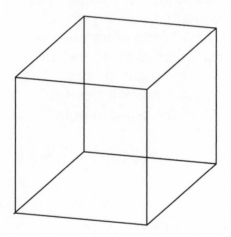

Answer to page 220

The missing number is **69**.
Multiply the first two numbers in each row, then
add 1 to determine the third number.

byTerry Stickels

In the figure below, one of the shaded areas is incorrect and one of the white areas is incorrect. When the two are switched, the whole figure is correct. Can you figure out which two should be switched?

17	54	3	19	28
12	63	6	32	90
34	45	50	22	55
39	29	21	33	48
37	15	60	7	40

Answer to page 221

30 students are majoring in both. If 72% of the 100 students are business majors, then 28% are not. If 58% are math majors, then 42% are not. So 28 + 42, or 70%, are not majoring in both.

 [sic].

by**Terry Stickels**

Here's a "trickle-down" puzzle. The rules are simple: You merely change one letter on each line to make a new word and continue until you reach the final word.

Now try this one:

BLOWS

_____

_____

_____

_____

GRASP

Answer to page 222

There are **18** different sets of parallel lines in a cube. Don't forget the diagonals!

by Terry Stickels

Can you determine the missing number in
the sequence below?

13   57   91   11   31   51   ?

Answer to page 223

Switch **33** and **22**.
The white areas are all divisible by 3,
but the shaded areas are not.

Can you divide the figure below into four equal parts?

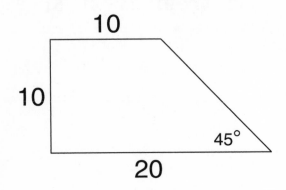

10

10

45°

20

Answer to page 224

Here's one way to solve this trickle-down:

BLOWS
GLOWS
GROWS
GROSS
GRASS
GRASP

How many cubes are missing from the
larger cube in the figure below?

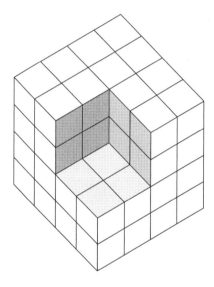

Answer to page 225

The next number would be **71**. If you place the
numbers closer together, you notice that these are
simply odd numbers in successive order.
1 3 5 7 9 11 13 15 17 1(9)

by**Terry Stickels**

What is the largest number that is spelled without any repeating letters?

Answer to page 226

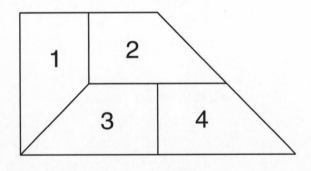

What number should replace the question
mark in the sequence below?

5 12 14 7 10 ? 13 6 8 15

Answer to page 227

9 cubes are missing.
8 small cubes and one large cube.

What should be the next number in the sequence below?

1 4 3 11 15 13 17 24 ?

Answer to page 228

FIVE THOUSAND is the largest number that can be spelled without repeating any letters.

Twenty-nine days ago Roger left for a trip that
lasted three days after that day he had left.
He then left the next day for a second trip that
lasted four days including the day he left.
He rested the next day.
If today is Wednesday, what day did he rest?

Answer to page 229

The missing number is **10**.
The sequence works from the outside in.

$$5 + 15 = 20$$
$$12 + 8 = 20$$
$$14 + 6 = 20$$
$$7 + 13 = 20$$
$$10 + ? = 20$$

How many different ways can four
cubes be put together, and what
does each way look like?

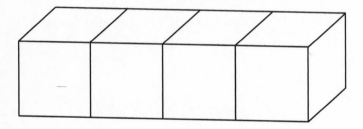

Answer to page 230

The next number is **23**.
The sequence is determined by how many
letters are in the spelling of the number.

The first two scales below are in perfect balance. How many circles should go in the question-marked box to make it balance perfectly?

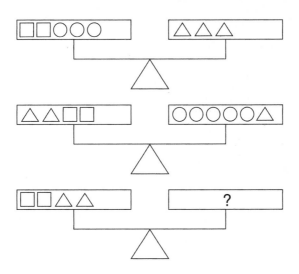

Answer to page 231

Roger rested on **WEDNESDAY**.

Which of the unfolded cubes would
fold into the cube to their right?

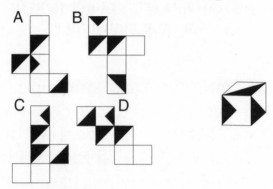

Answer to page 232

There are seven ways to put four cubes together. In addition to the figure shown in the question, here are the other six combinations:

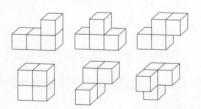

On the left are names that describe occupations.
The occupations are scrambled on the right.
Can you match them?

1. **CLARK**
2. **GROVER**
3. **SHERMAN**
4. **TURNER**
5. **WARREN**

a. lathe worker
b. parish clerk
c. overseer of game
d. miner of lead
e. cloth cutter

Answer to page 233

Seven circles are necessary to make the
third figure balance perfectly.

(Each circle counts as 2, each triangle
counts as 4, and each square counts as 3.)

by**Terry Stickels**

Can you determine the next two
numbers in the sequence below?

21 21 20 22 18 24 15 27 11 31 6 ? ?

Answer to page 234

Figure **B** folds into the cube depicted.

by Terry Stickels

Find the next number in this sequence.
Hint: Give it some time.

255

205

110

1210

1105

?

Answer to page 235

CLARK - parish clerk
GROVER - miner of lead
SHERMAN - cloth cutter
TURNER - lathe worker
WARREN - overseer of game

Can you determine why the letters of the alphabet are listed in the order below?

E T A O N R I S H D L U C M

F G Y P W B V K X J Q Z

Answer to page 236

The missing numbers are **36** and **0**.
There are really two sequences in the puzzle.
Starting with the first 21 and skipping every other
number, you'll notice the difference is 2, then 3,
then 4, then 5. Starting with the second 21 and
skipping every other number, you'll notice that the
difference is 1, then 2, then 3, then 4, etc.

by**Terry Stickels**

Here's an alphametic that will remind you
that spring is right around the corner.
Can you find the numbers that represent
each letter to make this math equation work?

$$
\begin{array}{r}
\text{BASE} \\
+ \ \text{BALL} \\
\hline
\text{GAMES}
\end{array}
$$

Answer to page 237

955, which is really 9:55 in the time sequence.
Starting with 2:55 and going backward
to 2:05 is 50 minutes. Then the difference
increases 5 minutes each time
(55 mins., 1 hr., 1 hr. 5 mins, 1 hr. 10 mins).

How many individual cubes are in the figure below? (All rows and columns run to completion unless you actually see them end.)

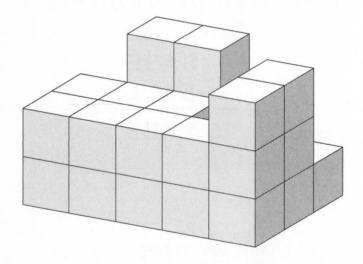

Answer to page 238

The order represents the letters' frequency of use in the English language, from most to least.

by**Terry Stickels**

Three of the four figures below can be drawn
without lifting a pencil, or crossing or going
over other lines. Which figure doesn't belong
with the others?

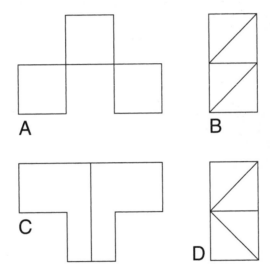

A   B

C   D

Answer to page 239

$$
\begin{array}{r}
7483 \\
+7455 \\
\hline
14938
\end{array}
$$

by**Terry Stickels** [sic].

As far as we can tell, there are only
two words that begin with *ANT* and
end with *ANT*. One word is
ANTIOXIDANT.
Can you figure out the other?

ANT _ _ _ _ _ _ _ ANT

Answer to page 240

30 individual cubes.

by**Terry Stickels**

Can you determine what number should replace the question mark in the figure below?

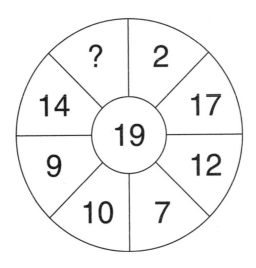

Answer to page 241

Figure **D** is the only one that cannot be drawn without lifting a pencil, or crossing or going over other lines.

by**Terry Stickels**

Here's a "trickle-down" puzzle. The rules are simple: You merely change one letter on each line to make a new word and continue until you reach the final word.

Now try
this one:

STUNT

_____

_____

_____

_____

PAIRS

Answer to page 242

The word is **ANTICOAGULANT**.

**A group of crows is often referred
to as a "murder of crows."
Can you match the animals below to
their appropriate grouping?**

1. RACEHORSES	a. convocation
2. EAGLES	b. mustering
3. GULLS	c. dray
4. SQUIRRELS	d. colony
5. STORKS	e. string

Answer to page 243

The missing number is **5**.
Each pair of numbers, starting with the 2 and the
17 and then moving clockwise, add up to 19.

A word and its anagram are used to complete the sentences below. Here's an example:

The building was of R E C E N T construction, but the cement had been of poor quality and the C E N T E R was crumbling.

The entire coalition of the country's _ _ _ _ _ _ rallied together and chanted their demands in _ _ _ _ _ _ so the nation would sympathize with their deplorable working conditions.

Answer to page 244

Here's one way to solve this trickle-down:

STUNT
STINT
SAINT
PAINT
PAINS
PAIRS

by**Terry Stickels**

Can you determine the two missing numbers at the end of the sequence below?

1 4 9
1 6 2
5 3 6
4 9 6
4 8 1
1 ? ?

Answer to page 245

RACEHORSES - string
EAGLES - convocation
GULLS - colony
SQUIRRELS - dray
STORKS - mustering

Below are three puzzles where, when a word
is added to the middle, it forms a front-end
word and a back-end word.
Example: ever GREEN house

PEAS _ _ _ ARCTIC

COME _ _ _ _ STAGE

FLASH _ _ _ _ _ HOUSE

Answer to page 246

The missing words are:
UNIONS and **UNISON**

Can you fill in the black boxes in figure D?

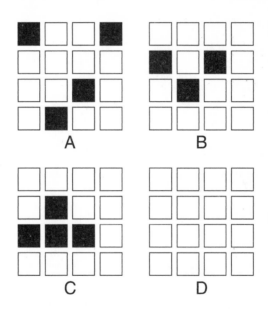

A   B

C   D

Answer to page 247

The missing numbers are **0** and **0**. These are
consecutive square numbers, beginning with 1,
and grouped three digits at a time.

<u>1 4 9</u> <u>16 25 36</u> <u>49 64 81</u> **<u>100</u>**

Can you unscramble
the word below?

WEEEDDILBR

Answer to page 248

peas **ANT** arctic
come **BACK** stage
flash **LIGHT** house

The first number to have its factors
add up to be more than itself is 12
(6, 4, 3, 2, 1). This doesn't include the
number itself. Quickly now, what are the next
three numbers for which this can be said?

Answer to page 249

The blackened square in the first column moves down one box in each successive grid. The square in the second column moves up one box in each grid. The square in the third column moves back and forth between the box to the left of it and the box it's in. The square in the fourth column moves down diagonally to the left.

by Terry Stickels

Here's one that ought to keep you
busy for a while ...

**Using four 4's and any
math symbols you like,
can you create an equation
that equals 19?**

Answer to page 250

The unscrambled word is:

BEWILDERED

by Terry Stickels

Below is a puzzle called a cryptarithm,
where the letters substitute for numbers.
Only one rule: No letter that starts a word
can be a zero.

T E N

T E N

+ F O R T Y

━━━━━━━━━

S I X T Y

Answer to page 251

18 (9, 6, 3, 2, 1)
20 (10, 5, 4, 2, 1)
24 (12, 8, 6, 4, 3, 2, 1)

Here's another tough number problem ...

**If our number system were
based on "6" instead of "10," how
would you write the number 13?
How would you write 13
if our number system
were based on "9"?**

Answer to page 252

Here's one way. Were you able to find another?
4! - 4 - (4/4) = 19

byTerry Stickels

**Let's see if you can wrap your mind
around this one ...**

**If you total the ages of Bob
and Bill, you get 50.
Ten years ago Bob was
twice as old as Bill.
How old are they now?**

Answer to page 253

$$
\begin{array}{r}
850 \\
850 \\
+\,29786 \\
\hline
31486
\end{array}
$$

**If Alex's son is my son's father,
what am I to Alex?**

HIS GRANDFATHER
I AM ALEX
HIS GRANDSON
HIS SON
HIS FATHER

Answer to page 254

In base 6, **21** is the same as our 13.
In base 9, **14** is the same as our 13.

STICKELERS

The missing letter in the middle of the figure below completes each of the four scrambled words in the four quadrants. Can you determine the missing letter and unscramble each word?

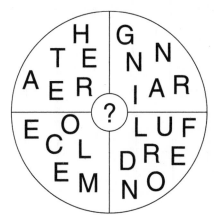

Answer to page 255

Bob is **30** and Bill is **20**. Ten years ago the sum of their ages would be 30, which means Bob would have to be 20 and Bill 10 if Bob were twice Bill's age.

by **Terry Stickels**

Try to keep up with me on this one ...

In a room, there are six brown-eyed brunettes. If all together there are 15 brunettes, nine people with brown eyes, and three people who are neither brown-eyed nor brunette, how many people are in the room?

Answer to page 256

I am Alex's **SON**.

**Can you unscramble the letters
below to form a word?**

M

M O A R T

C E N E G

L E S T I

Answer to page 257

The missing letter is **W**.
The unscrambled words are:
WEATHER
WARNING
WELCOME
WONDERFUL

by **Terry Stickels**

Below are three puzzles where, when a word
is added to the middle, it forms a front-end
word and a back-end word.
Example: ever GREEN house

TEAM _ _ _ _ SHOP

SLING _ _ _ _ GUN

HENCE _ _ _ _ _ RIGHT

Answer to page 258

There are a total of
21 people in the room.

In the sentence below, a word and its anagram are used to complete the sentence. Can you fill in the blanks with the appropriate words?

The slightly eccentric and often wrong mathematician _ _ _ _ _ _ _ that he had found a new way to write numbers in the _ _ _ _ _ _ _ system.

Answer to page 259

The unscrambled word is:
ELECTROMAGNETISM

by**Terry Stickels**

Below is a grid where all rows, columns and diagonals each add up to 41.
Can you fill in the missing numbers?

2			26
		5	
	1		
9			4

Answer to page 260

team **WORK** shop
sling **SHOT** gun
hence **FORTH** right

Can you determine the missing number in box E?

4	21
7	12

A

5	4
1	20

B

2	55
11	10

C

13	36
6	78

D

16	?
2	112

E

Answer to page 261

The missing words are:
CLAIMED & DECIMAL

 [sic]. ─────

byTerry Stickels

Can you determine what number should come next in the sequence below?

1	84
8	85
11	86
18	87
80	88
81	89
82	100
83	?

Answer to page 262

2	7	6	26
10	18	5	8
20	1	17	3
9	15	13	4

by **Terry Stickels**

There is only one 15-letter word that can be
spelled without repeating a letter.
Can you guess the word?

U _ _ _ _ _ _ _ _ _ _ _ _ _ E

Answer to page 263

The missing number is **14**.
In each box, the diagonal numbers are whole
multiples of each other. In box A, the multiple
is 3. In box B, the multiple is 4. In box C, the
multiple is 5. In box D, the multiple is 6.
In box E, the multiple is 7.

by**Terry Stickels**

Assuming all rows and columns come to an end unless you actually see them end, how many individual cubes are in the figure below?

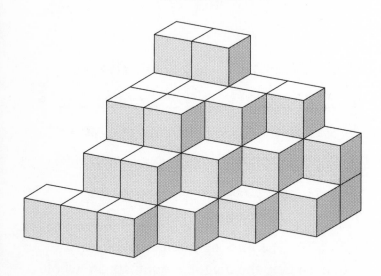

Answer to page 264

The next number should be **101**.
These are the numbers, in order, starting with one, that begin with a vowel.

by **Terry Stickels**

Below are five numbered words,
each describing a particular shape.
Can you match the numbered words with
their correct meanings to the right?

1. ERUCIFORM   a. web-shaped

2. TEXTIFORM   b. sword-shaped

3. ENSIFORM   c. sickle-shaped

4. SULCIFORM   d. caterpillar-shaped

5. FALCIFORM   e. grooved or

                     depression shape

Answer to page 265

The only 15-letter word that can be
spelled without repeating a letter is:
UNCOPYRIGHTABLE

 [sic].

by**Terry Stickels**

Below is an incomplete sentence containing
two seven-letter words that are anagrams
of one another. I'll give you the
first two letters of each word.
Can you determine the missing words?

The **HO** _ _ _ _ _ threatened to

SH _ _ _ _ _ the picnic — there

must've been 500 of them.

Answer to page 266
45 individual cubes.

 [sic].

by**Terry Stickels**

Can you determine which one of the five figures below does not belong with the others?

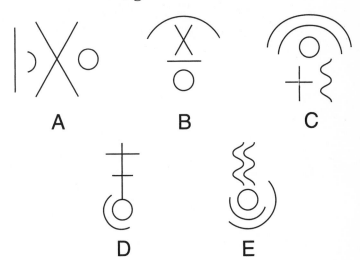

A   B   C

D   E

Answer to page 267
Here are the correct pairings:
1-d; 2-a; 3-b; 4-e; 5-c

by**Terry Stickels**

**Below are three "squeezer" puzzles.
Can you find the correct word to be placed in the
middle to create two new words, one on the front
end and one on the back end?
Here's an example of how it works:**

ever <u>GREEN</u> horn

mast _ _ _ _ strong

seven _ _ _ _ age

grand _ _ _ _ _ still

Answer to page 268

The two missing words are:
HORNETS and **SHORTEN**

by **Terry Stickels**

Here's a "trickle-down" puzzle. The rules are simple: You merely change one letter on each line to make a new word and continue until you reach the final word.

Now try this one:

FLUSH

———

———

———

———

BRATS

Answer to page 269

Figure **E** does not belong with the others. It is the only figure that doesn't contain a straight line.

by **Terry Stickels**

See if you can follow me on this one ...

On a certain street there are 31 houses. Twelve of those houses have fewer than seven rooms. Ten of those houses have more than eight rooms. Eight of those houses have more than nine rooms. What is the total number of houses that have seven, eight or nine rooms?

Answer to page 270

mast **HEAD** strong
seven **TEEN** age
grand **STAND** still

byTerry Stickels

Can you crack the code, and
determine the hidden message below?

GUVF CHMMYR VFA'G
GUNG QVSSVPHYG!

Answer to page 271

Here's one way   FLUSH
to solve this   BLUSH
trickle-down: BRUSH
                  BRASH
                  BRASS
                  BRATS

Can you determine the missing numbers in the figure below?

5	6
2	4

is to

20	12
7	10

as

1	3
7	8

is to

?	?
8	?

Answer to page 272

The total number of houses
with 7, 8 or 9 rooms is **11**.

by **Terry Stickels**

Can you figure out what
number should come next
in the sequence below?

1 1 2 6 24 120 720 ?

Answer to page 273

The code reads:
THIS PUZZLE ISN'T THAT DIFFICULT
The code is found by cutting the alphabet
in half and using the opposite letters.
A B C D E F G H I J K L M
N O P Q R S T U V W X Y Z

by **Terry Stickels**

Can you figure out which of the
following sentences does not belong
with the others?

1. I'm out with angina.

2. Omaha has interesting offerings.

3. Only ranked entrants go on next.

4. We all enjoy barbecue and baseball.

Answer to page 274

8	21
8	11

- Multiply the numbers diagonally
  to get the upper numbers
  (e.g., 1 x 8 = 8; 7 x 3 = 21).
- Add the two left-hand numbers
  together to get the lower left number.
- Add the two right-hand numbers
  to get the lower right number.

**Can you find at least one anagram
for the word below?**

UNDERLYING

Answer to page 275

The next number is **5040**.

$$1 \times 1 = 1$$
$$1 \times 2 = 2$$
$$2 \times 3 = 6$$
$$6 \times 4 = 24$$
$$24 \times 5 = 120$$
$$120 \times 6 = 720$$
$$720 \times 7 = 5040$$

Below is an incomplete sentence
containing two six-letter words
that are anagrams of one another.
Can you determine the missing words?

The ambassador was going

to need a police _ _ _ _ _ _

for that particular _ _ _ _ _ _

of the country.

Answer to page 276

Sentence **4** does not belong. The other sentences
each spell out the name of a state with the first
letter of each word.

1. IOWA
2. OHIO
3. OREGON

There are four words commonly used in
English that end in vous.
Two of them are
MISCHIEVOUS and NERVOUS.
Can you come up with the other two?

Answer to page 277

An anagram for UNDERLYING is:
ENDURINGLY

by**Terry Stickels**

**Can you match the words on top
with their meanings below?**

1. VANGUARD
2. WRAITH
3. OSSIFY
4. RATHSKELLER
5. CRINOLINE

a. An underground bar or restaurant
b. To change into bone
c. A ghost
d. The leaders in a movement
e. A coarse, stiff cloth

Answer to page 278

The missing words are:
ESCORT and **SECTOR**

Here's an alphametic that is also a tribute
to one of baseball's great pitchers ...
Each letter stands for a number, and no word
can begin with zero. For this puzzle, let O = 2.
Can you find the numbers that represent
each letter to make this math equation work?

$$
\begin{array}{r}
\text{N E W} \\
\text{Y O R K} \\
+ \ \text{Y A N K} \\
\hline
\text{F O R D}
\end{array}
$$

Answer to page 279

The other two words are:
GRIEVOUS and **RENDEZVOUS**

by**Terry Stickels**

Here's a brain-twister:

If it were 3 hours later than it is now, it would be twice as long until midnight as it would be if it were four hours later. What time is it now?

Answer to page 280

1 - d
2 - c
3 - b
4 - a
5 - e

Which of the words below does not
belong with the others?

a) SPAGHETTI
b) PASTTIME
c) DUMBELL
d) COMMITED
e) HARRANGUE

Answer to page 281

```
    806
   3259
 + 3189
  ─────
   7254
```

What one fraction is represented by the shaded areas in the square below?

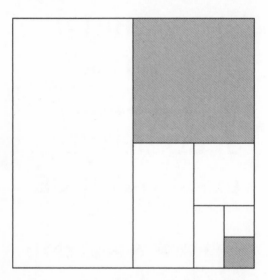

Answer to page 282

It is **7:00** pm.

**Below are anagrams of the
names of three NBA stars.
Can you unscramble them?**

1) JAM LOB SNEER

2) OVERALL NINES

3) NO MYTH AN ORACLE

Answer to page 283

SPAGHETTI does not belong
with the others. All of the other
words are misspelled.

by Terry Stickels

**The letters in the grid below are strung together
in such a way that they spell a word.
Can you determine the word?**

N	O	I
L	O	S
P	X	E

Answer to page 284

The shaded areas account for **17/64** of the whole square.
Here's one way to look at the solution:
The larger shaded area is 1/4 the whole square. Each
area, going down in size, is half its predecessor. When
you finally get down to the smallest shaded area, you
realize it is 1/64 the whole square. 1/64 + 1/4
(or 16/64) = 17/64.

by **Terry Stickels**

Below is an *alphametic*, or *cryptarithm*, where each letter stands for a number. No word can begin with a zero, and the same letter always retains the same value. Can you determine what numbers should replace each letter?

$$
\begin{array}{r}
\text{T W O} \\
\text{T H R E E} \\
+ \text{S E V E N} \\
\hline
\text{T W E L V E}
\end{array}
$$

Answer to page 285

The three names are:
LEBRON JAMES
ALLEN IVERSON
CARMELO ANTHONY

by Terry Stickels

Below are three different word puzzles.
Try them with friends and family!

1) The longest word in the English language that contains only one vowel is nine letters long. What is the word?

2) The words TYPEWRITER and REPERTOIRE, each 10 letters, are part of a group of words that are the longest words that can be spelled using the top row of a typewriter. Can you name one more? (There may be more than one answer.)

3) What is the only anagram for the word MONDAY?

Answer to page 286

The hidden word is **EXPLOSION**. Starting in the lower right-hand corner, zigzag back and forth, from bottom to top, to find the answer.

What letter should come next in the sequence below?

H I N O S X ?

Answer to page 287

1 0 6		1 0 4
1 9 7 2 2	OR	1 9 7 2 2
+ 8 2 5 2 4		+ 8 2 5 2 6
1 0 2 3 5 2		1 0 2 3 5 2

Can you determine what the missing letters are in the figures below?

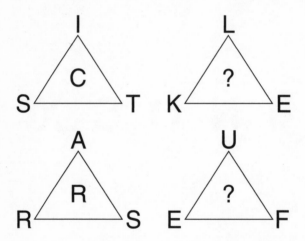

Answer to page 288

1) STRENGTHS
2) PROPRIETOR
3) DYNAMO

If you have the same amount of pennies and nickels and no other coins, which of the money amounts below is the only possible amount you can have?

a) **$ .49**
b) **$ .91**
c) **$ .36**
d) **$ .45**

Answer to page 289

The missing letter is **Z**.
The group represents all the letters that read the same right-side up and upside down.

**How many anagrams can you find
for the word *nameless*?**

NAMELESS

Answer to page 290

The missing letters are **E** and **N**.
Starting with the lower left-hand letter in the first triangle
and going around it counterclockwise, then to the middle,
then on to the next triangle, the phrase reads:
STICKELERS ARE FUN

by**Terry Stickels**

Based on the five phrases below, can you assign numbers 1 through 4 to each of the four names mentioned?

- If Laura is not 2, then Nick is not 3
- If Marty is either 3 or 4, then Laura is 2
- If Nick is not 1, then Marty is 4
- If Ollie is 3, then Marty is not 2
- If Ollie is not 2, then Marty is 2

Answer to page 291

The answer is **C** — 36 cents.

Because a penny and a nickel add up to 6 cents, and you have equal amounts of both, your answer must be divisible by 6. 36 was the only choice divisible by 6.

by **Terry Stickels**

Here is a "trickle-down" puzzle. The rules
are simple: Change one letter on each
line to make a new word and continue
until you reach the final word.

Try this one:

BELLY

——

——

——

TOOTS

Answer to page 292

We found four. How about you?

LAMENESS

MALENESS

MANELESS

SALESMAN

Below are three "squeezer" puzzles.
Can you find the correct word to be placed in
the middle of each to create two new words,
one front-end, one back-end?
Here's an example of how it works:

ever <u>G R E E N</u> horn

top _ _ _ _ tail

ram _ _ _ _ ridge

safe _ _ _ _ _ rail

Answer to page 293

Nick – 1
Marty – 2
Laura – 3
Ollie – 4

by Terry Stickels

Can you match the phrases on the left with their anagrammed phrases on the right?

1. **Election results**

2. **Payment received**

3. **The hurricanes**

4. **William Shakespeare**

5. **Emperor Octavian**

a. I'll make a wise phrase

b. Captain over Rome

c. Every cent paid me

d. Lies — let's recount

e. These churn air

Answer to page 294

Here's one way to solve this trickle-down puzzle:

BELLY
BELLS
TELLS
TOLLS
TOOLS
TOOTS

by **Terry Stickels**

There is an old puzzle that asks you to place four nickels and four pennies within a 4x4 grid in such a way that no two coins of the same denomination will be next to each other in the same row, horizontally, vertically, or diagonally. Below is the answer that is usually given. Now, can you come up with at least one other solution?

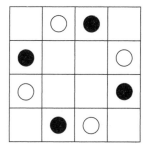

Answer to page 295

top **COAT** tail
ram **PART** ridge
safe **GUARD** rail

 [sic].

byTerry Stickels

On a digital clock, like the face of one below, there are 28 line segments to represent the time — of course, not all are used at the same time. One of these segments is used more than any other one. Can you determine which one it is?

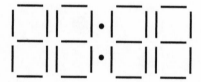

Answer to page 296

1 - d
2 - c
3 - e
4 - a
5 - b

by Terry Stickels

[sic].

If I start you out with three sticks, then give you an additional six sticks, can you create ten?

|

|

|

Answer to page 297

Here's one way to solve this puzzle.
Can you find another one?

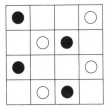

by**Terry Stickels**

Can you fill in the missing numbers in the figure below?

1
1 1
2 1
1 2 1 1
1 1 1 2 2 1
? ? ? ? ? ?

Answer to page 298

The segment in the lower right of the last number is used more than any other.

Five of the six pairs of letters are grouped in a logical manner that is consistent for all five groupings. Can you determine which pair does not belong with the others?

CI GM PV

BH TY NT

Answer to page 299

Here's one way to take 3 sticks
and add 6 sticks to make ten!

by**Terry Stickels**

**Each figure below follows the same logic
to determine the number in the middle.
Can you determine the missing number
in figure E?**

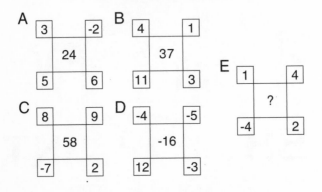

Answer to page 300

The missing numbers are: **3 1 2 2 1 1**.
This is determined by saying the numbers aloud for each
preceding row beginning with the first 1: one one (which is
now the second row), then two ones (which is now the third
row), etc. The row after the missing row would read:
1 3 1 1 2 2 2 1
Get it?

by**Terry Stickels**

Here's a "trickle-down" puzzle. The rules are simple: You merely change one letter on each line to make a new word and continue until you reach the final word.

Try this one:

MINOR

_____

_____

_____

_____

DUDES

Answer to page 301

The **TY** grouping does not belong with the others. They have four letters between them, alphabetically, where as the others have five.

**What number logically comes
next in the following sequence?**

4 6 9 5 4 2 3 9 ?

Answer to page 302

The missing number is **-4**.
To get this, multiply the top two numbers in each
box and add to the bottom two numbers (also
multiplied) to determine the middle number.

by Terry Stickels

Can you determine what letter should replace the question mark in the figure below?

E	E	N	S
2	5	6	1

U	?	Q	C
4	8	3	7

Answer to page 303

Here's one way to solve this trickle-down puzzle:

MINOR
MINER
DINER
DINES
DUNES
DUDES

One straight line can divide a circle into two parts. Two straight lines can divide it into four parts. What is the maximum number of pieces created with four straight cuts?

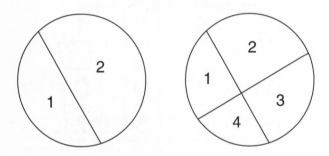

Answer to page 304

The next number is **8**.
The numbers represent the number of letters in each word of the question.
Sequence has **8** letters.

by **Terry Stickels**

Below are three "squeezer" puzzles.
Can you find the correct word to be placed in
the middle of each to create two new words,
one front-end, one back-end?
Here's an example of how it works:

ever <u>G R E E N</u> horn

ring _ _ _ _ hole

tomb _ _ _ _ _ wall

car _ _ _ _ table

Answer to page 305

The missing letter is **E**.
The numbers in each box indicate the order the
boxes should be placed in. Once in order, they
spell out SEQUENCE — the missing letter
being "E."

STICKELERS [sic].

by**Terry Stickels**

How many words can you make from the word QUARTER? We came up with 23, but there are more! Can you beat 20 words to become an expert?

Rules: You can only use a letter as often as it appears in the word itself, but you don't have to use all of the letters (ex: the word RATE is an acceptable answer).

QUARTER

Answer to page 306

With four straight cuts to a circle, the maximum number of pieces made is **11**.

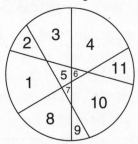

[sic].

byTerry Stickels

How quickly can you get this one?

**If 2 typists can type 2 pages
in 2 minutes, how many typists
will it take to type 20 pages
in 4 minutes?**

Answer to page 307

ring **WORM** hole
tomb **STONE** wall
car **POOL** table

STICKELERS [sic].

by**Terry Stickels**

You may know that a tetrahedron has four faces and six edges, and a cube has six faces and 12 edges, but can you tell me how many edges a twelve-faced dodecahedron has?

Answer to page 308

Here are the 23 we came up with:

RATE	TEA	TRUE	EAR	ARE
ATE	EAT	TRUER	TARE	RUT
QUART	AT	RUE	ERR	REAR
RAT	A	TEAR	ERA	
TAR	RARE	ART	QUA	

Did you find more?

by Terry Stickels

Is the statement below true or false?

**Elizabeth's niece's father's
daughter's aunt could be
Elizabeth.**

Answer to page 309

It will take **10** typists to type
20 pages in 4 minutes.

by **Terry Stickels**

This one is easier than you think ...

Yesterday is three days before the day that is three days before Sunday. What is today?

Answer to page 310

A twelve-faced dodecahedron has **30** edges.

by **Terry Stickels**

In the sentence below, a word and its anagram are used to complete it. Here's an example:

The building was of <u>R E C E N T</u> construction, but the cement had been of poor quality and the <u>C E N T E R</u> was crumbling.

The enthusiasm of the crowd at an _ _ _ _ _ _ _ can carry you away, so be sure to exercise _ _ _ _ _ _ _ .

Answer to page 311

The statement is **TRUE**.

by**Terry Stickels**

If the cube below is painted red, and it is cut into cubes as shown by the lines, how many cubes have no sides painted at all?

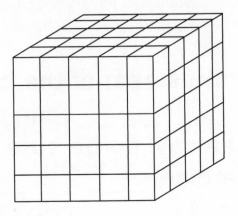

Answer to page 312

Today is **TUESDAY**.

by**Terry Stickels**

Below are three "squeezer" puzzles.
Can you find the correct word to be placed in
the middle of each to creat two new words,
one front-end, one back-end?
Here's an example of how it works:

ever <u>G R E E N</u> horn

trade _ _ _ _ breaker

pea _ _ _ shell

militia _ _ _ tally

Answer to page 313

The missing words are:
AUCTION and **CAUTION**

315

by Terry Stickels

The relationship of the two numbers in each block is the same for each block.
Based on that knowledge, can you determine the missing number in the last block?

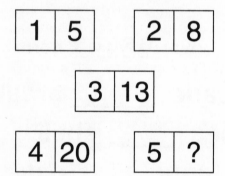

Answer to page 314

27 cubes are not painted. The figure is 5x5x5 which means there are a total of 125 cubes. The inside cube that contains no painted cubes is 3x3x3 which equals 27.

by**Terry Stickels**

[sic].

Consider these facts ...

Ally, Brian, Carly and Dan went fishing. Dan caught more than Carly. Ally and Brian together caught exactly the same number of fish that Carly and Dan caught together. Ally and Dan did not catch as many as Brian and Carly.

Based on the information provided above, can you list the four names of the fishing crew in order, from most to least fish caught?

Answer to page 315

trade **WIND** breaker
pea **NUT** shell
militia **MEN** tally

by**Terry Stickels**

Based on the information provided in the scales below, can you determine how many circles will balance the 2 squares in the last scale?

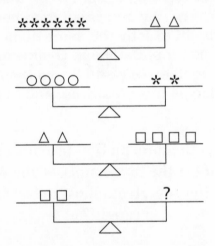

Answer to page 316

The missing number is **29**.
The first number in each block is squared, then
4 is added to arrive at the second number.

Below is an anagram of the name of one
of the most famous men in history.
Can you unscramble it?

NEST IN BARE LITE

Answer to page 317

Here's the order from most to least caught:
Brian, Dan, Carly, Ally

by**Terry Stickels** [sic].

Can you determine which of the choices
(a through e) should come after the word
RAINBOW?

PLAYFUL
FULFILL
FILLING
INGRAIN
RAINBOW
?

a) BENCHMARK **b)** BOWLING **c)** LAVENDER

d) SIMPLE **e)** MASTER

Answer to page 318

It would take **6** circles
to balance the 2 squares.

Here's a "trickle-down" puzzle. The rules are
simple: You merely change one letter on each
line to make a new word and continue
until you reach the final word.

Try this one:

CROWD

———

———

———

———

GLASS

Answer to page 319

The unscrambled anagram reads:
ALBERT EINSTEIN

Can you determine the missing number in the sequence below?

5 12 14 7 10 17
13 6 5 12 1 ?

Answer to page 320

BOWLING should come next. Starting with PLAYFUL, the last few letters of each word are the beginning letters of the following word.

by**Terry Stickels**

**Here's a trick you can play with your friends
to see who can solve the problem the fastest!**

From a pile of 50 pennies,
50 nickels and 50 dimes, select
16 coins which have a total value of 50
cents. In your selection, you must use at
least one penny, one nickel and one dime.

Answer to page 321

Here's one way
to solve this
trickle-down
puzzle:

CROWD
CROWS
CROSS
GROSS
GRASS
GLASS

by **Terry Stickels**

Can you determine which one of the five words below does not belong with the others?

COUPON
OVERSTUFFED
REDCAP
FEDERAL
ABUTS

Answer to page 322

The next number is **-6**.
Each pair of numbers, beginning with 5 and 12, show a pattern where the difference is:
7, -7, 7, -7, etc.

by **Terry Stickels**

Here's some trivia for you:

How many states lie adjacent to Tennessee, and can you name them?

Answer to page 323

10 pennies
4 nickels
2 dimes
Can you find other combinations?

by**Terry Stickels**

Below are three "squeezer" puzzles.
Can you find the correct word to be placed in
the middle of each to create two new words,
one front-end and one back-end?
Here's an example of how it works:

ever <u>GREEN</u> horn

hour _ _ _ _ _ ware

rock _ _ _ _ out

sir _ _ _ _ cloth

Answer to page 324

OVERSTUFFED does not belong with the
others. It has four consecutive letters of the
alphabet forward, whereas the others have three
consecutive letters backward.

by **Terry Stickels**

What four-letter word can be put at the beginning of the three words and at the end of the other three words to form six new words?

_ _ _ _ **worn**

_ _ _ _ **piece**

_ _ _ _ **keeper**

down _ _ _ _

some _ _ _ _

bed _ _ _ _

Answer to page 325

There are 8. Starting with Kentucky to the north and moving clockwise, you have Virginia, North Carolina, Georgia, Alabama, Mississippi, Arkansas, and Missouri.

by**Terry Stickels** [sic].

Below are five four-digit
numbers that are the same right-side up
as they are upside-down. What is the next
four-digit number in the sequence?

6009   6119   6699

6889   6969   ?

Answer to page 326

hour **GLASS** ware
rock **FALL** out
sir **LOIN** cloth

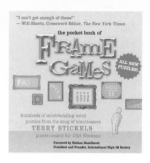

THE POCKET BOOK OF FRAME GAMES
By Terry Stickels
ISBN-13: 978-1-59233-195-6
ISBN-10: 1-59233-091-5
$9.95/£4.99/$13.95 CAN
Paperback; 208 pages
Available wherever books are sold.

"I can't get enough of these!"
—Will Shortz, Crossword Editor *New York Times*

It's more than just a pretty picture—it's a complete cranial workout!

This innovative collection of Frame Games is a blast of fresh air for your brain! Within the decorative border of each framed puzzle lies a clever arrangement of letters, words, shapes, and symbols illustrating a well-known concept or saying. Your job is to look carefully, examine the relationships within the frame, and determine the meaning. Think of it as graphic shorthand: A picture of a branch lying between the letters "M" and "UD" means "stick in the mud"! An array of uneven numbers next to the word "ends"? "Odds and ends," of course! Great for bathroom reading, train reading, and those lazy Sunday mornings, this book includes hundreds of mind-boggling puzzles to get those synapses firing!

THE LITTLE BOOK OF BATHROOM SUDOKU

Terry Stickels
ISBN - 13: 978-1-59233-219-9
ISBN - 10: 1-59233-219-6
$9.95/£4.99/$13.95 CAN
Available wherever books are sold.

"Terry Stickels' puzzle books are great!
He's always finding new ways to test our logic. This collection
is as enjoyable as it is challenging."
—Pat Battagalia, Author of *Are You Smart, or What?*
*A Bizarre Book of Games and Fun for Everyone and So You
Think You're Smart, 150 Fun and Challenging Brain Teasers*

160 All-New Puzzles You Can Do in the Loo!

Sudoku is the most intensely addictive puzzle available, and with good reason—it's fun, it requires no math or knowledge of trivia, and is a great way to test your logic skills on the train, on the plane, or even in the bathroom!

With 160 puzzles of varying degrees of difficulty—from easy to evil—this book is the ideal companion for puzzle lovers of all ages and skill levels. By figuring out how to place numbers in a grid so that each number appears in each row, square, and column of the grid, you can challenge your logical thinking.